THREE
SIMPLE
WORDS

THREE SIMPLE WORDS

*These words have changed the lives and
revolutionized the world for all who follow them.*

ED MALONE

REDEMPTION PRESS

Published by Redemption Press, PO Box 427, Enumclaw, WA 98022.

Toll-Free (844) 2REDEEM (273-3336)

Redemption Press is honored to present this title in partnership with the author. The views expressed or implied in this work are those of the author. Redemption Press provides our imprint seal representing design excellence, creative content, and high-quality production.

The author has tried to recreate events, locales, and conversations from memories of them. In order to maintain their anonymity, in some instances the names of individuals, some identifying characteristics, and some details may have been changed, such as physical properties, occupations, and places of residence.

Scripture quotations are from The ESV® Bible (The Holy Bible, English Standard Version®), copyright © 2001 by Crossway, a publishing ministry of Good News Publishers. Used by permission. All rights reserved.

ISBN 13: 978-1-64645-414-3 (Paperback)
978-1-64645-413-6 (ePub)
978-1-64645-415-0 (Mobi)

Library of Congress Catalog Card Number: 2021905055

DEDICATION

My mom, Jerry (Atkins) Malone, lived to be ninety-five years old. Her heart's desire to be a servant in our home, in her church, and in our community was inspiring. The way she lived out her faith provided a vivid example for my own journey.

During my childhood, times were tough and money was scarce. Even so, Mom persevered, trusted God, and never complained. We always had food to eat, clean clothes to wear, and a loving home kept to perfection. As a kid, I will never forget watching her washing clothes on the back porch using a wringer washing machine in the cold days of winter, causing her hands to split open from the exposure. Driven by love and her sense of responsibility, she did whatever was required to meet the needs of our family.

I never heard her say an unkind thing about anyone. I have seen her cry, but I never saw her express anger. She always had the strength of character to let things pass and give folks the benefit of the doubt. She was a remarkable person. More than anyone I've ever known, she lived daily the challenge Jesus gave: "It is more blessed to give than to receive." Her appreciation and love for our home was special. Her thankfulness for what she had rather than always wanting something more was a lesson in life she modeled that I will always treasure.

The way she lived was God-honoring, as it was her heart's desire to walk as Jesus walked. During the last two years of her life, suffering from dementia, she moved in with us. Due to her illness, Mom was quite confused and often afraid. Going to sleep at night was quite a challenge. To help her relax, I would sit with her each night reading from the Gospels for an extended period of time. Over the course of two years, we read through the Gospels multiple times, which served as the background for writing *Three Simple Words*. Her love for the Scriptures and the old hymns of the faith stayed with her even when she did not know my name.

Once when Mom was having a very confused and anxious day, we started walking down our half-mile-long driveway for her to find her way home. At one point she turned to me and said, "You are the preacher, and I have always loved you, right? Well, I am ready for you to take me to heaven." I responded, "Oh, how I wish I could, Mom, but we must each make our own journey. For sure, you have shown me the way. It is because of you that I know the realness of our heavenly Father's love. He's the one that will take you home."

Her ability to love unconditionally, her willingness to empty herself in serving others, and her genuine faith fulfilled God's desire and plan for her life. She was a God-honoring example of a life well lived. I admire who she was in God, and it is my ambition to follow the legacy she left behind. Mom modeled what it means to answer the call of Jesus: "Come, follow me."

CONTENTS

Giving Thanks

Barbara Ryan worked tirelessly over a period of many months, editing my many rewrites. Barbara's editorial help and encouragement enabled me to stay the course.

My opportunity to write was made possible by Christ's Community Church. Their desire to know and implement the things of God more fully has made it a pleasure to serve as their pastor. Much of what I have written was first hammered out in sermon form among this wonderful group of people.

My wife, Gale, graced me with patience as this project extended over several years. Each announcement that I had completed the final edit was met with a smile and the response, "I've heard that before." She was right.

Every book needs a publisher in order to move from the computer to something you are now holding in your hand. In completion of the final step in this process, Redemption Press added their exceptional experience as a publishing house to package *Three Simple Words* into its final form. Their personal involvement and excitement in working with me was a blessing.

WELCOME

SINCE THE BEGINNING OF TIME, THE MIRACLE AND wonder of life have captivated the mind of humanity. The complexity of design, allowing for sight, human reasoning, and preservation of our physical existence, rests on intricate and fascinating phenomena. At a cosmic level, we live in a unique, finely tuned spot in our vast universe, allowing for life to exist. Alongside the marvel of our physical world, the desire for love in relationships, the capacity of self-awareness, and the moral press of conscience, there is a deeper side of life—the realm of the Spirit.

Humanity's attempt to understand the dimension of life that lies beyond the physical has created many questions—God or gods, are they evil or good, to be placated or enjoyed? Diverse proposals have been offered to explain the spiritual realm and the proper response to it.

Some consider the grandeur of life as a lucky, cosmic accident driven by blind chance. The mindset of others is captured in the Epicurean mantra of eat, drink, and be merry, for tomorrow you may die. Surely life has meaning beyond surviving as the smartest animal on our planet.

History reveals a continuous thread of religious expression being given to what most of humanity senses as a spiritual authority over life. The nation of Israel, led by the faith of Abraham, came into being centered around the belief of there being only one God. This monotheistic faith of the Israelites was a departure from the polytheistic concepts prevalent in their day. Israel's understanding of the one true and living God came as a result of his guiding their lives, caring for their needs, and redeeming them from life's circumstances.

Most forms of religion have a prescribed way of relating to the spiritual realm. Some go to the extreme of sacrificing their children to satisfy the gods. For Israel, the worship experience that was centered in the sacrificial system became primary. With extravagance and devotion to ritual, they offered sacrifices at the temple as what they thought mattered most to God.

The Old Testament prophet Micah challenged Israel with an important question: "With what shall I come before the LORD, and bow myself before God on high? Shall I come before him with burnt offerings, with calves a year old? Will the LORD be pleased with thousands of rams, with ten thousands of rivers of oil? Shall I give my firstborn for my transgression, the fruit of my body for the sin of my soul? He has told you, O man, what is good; and what does the LORD require of you but to do justice, and to love kindness, and to walk humbly with your God" (Mic. 6:6–8)?

Think for a moment of what life would be like if all of humanity lived by justice, kindness, and humility before God.

God's intention was for Israel to be a corrective to humanity's misunderstanding of the spiritual realm. Her commission was to bring the truth of God to the world. Instead, succeeding generations embraced religious practices of the cultures around them. God sent prophets calling for change. Their message was refused, and many of them were killed. Not listening to these prophets was one thing, but to feel the need to kill them in the name of their religion was extreme beyond measure.

The ultimate expression of God's desire for humanity to know the truth about him was expressed by Jesus coming to live in our world. At the time of his birth, Israel was still spiritually out of line with God. Jesus confronted their religious expression as empty lip service void of a heart connection with the Father. Even though he was the Son of God, Jesus was rejected by those proclaiming to be God's people, who called for his crucifixion as the enemy of God.

Christianity, dedicated to the truth Jesus revealed, emerged after his resurrection as the new way to live. For several centuries, Christianity was faithful to the call of Jesus even while enduring persecution. However, as with Israel, the passing of time brought change. The way of life taught by Jesus became absorbed in a man-made system of religious expression known as Catholicism, which set the standard for Christianity for more than one thousand years. In 1517, the Protestant Reformation was initiated as a bold statement of radical change being needed.

The warning of the apostle Paul to Timothy proved true: "For the time is coming when people will not endure sound teaching, but having itching ears they will accumulate for themselves teachers to suit their own passions, and will turn away from listening to the truth" (2 Tim. 4:3–4). Throughout the history of the Judeo-Christian faith, keeping God's people on course has been a continuous task.

The Christian movement known as Protestantism, birthed out of the Reformation, is now five hundred years old. During this time, division and theological shifts have occurred. It is critical to ask whether some groups within Protestantism have evolved into yet another man-made, lip-service expression of religion? During the past few decades, Christianity has seen significant changes. Are these changes good or bad, right or wrong? These questions are the most important questions of life.

For many, getting their response to God right is simple. They contend if one believes in God and tries to be good, everything will work out in the end. Against such thinking, the scribes and Pharisees believed in God, revered the Scriptures, and attended temple, yet Jesus announced that they were outside of the kingdom of heaven. Not being in the kingdom when they believed they were was tragic. Jesus expanded his warning by telling others that not all who say "Lord, Lord" will enter the kingdom, that those saved will be few, and that the way to life is through a narrow gate, which few will find. These warning statements given by Jesus come as quite a surprise. Few rather than many being saved is alarming.

How can something, which is a gift, be so hard to receive? Jesus announced that he came to give us life and give it abundantly. He also said, "Fear not, little flock, for it is your Father's good pleasure to give you the kingdom" (Luke 12:32). The problem is Jesus gives what humanity does not want. The fullness of life as defined by our selfishness is not what Jesus makes available. Jesus spoke with clarity of God's desire for humanity. We are no longer left to sort through man-made religious distortions. In the chapters that follow, a synopsis of his life is presented so that you can evaluate where you stand with who he is and his invitation to "Come, follow me."

A Word of Encouragement

The fullness of life extending into an endless future awaits those who choose to follow Jesus in a present, spiritual relationship of serving God now and for all of eternity. It is the meaning and purpose of our existence. Failure to make the proper response to what he makes available bears eternal consequences.

CHAPTER 1

COME, FOLLOW ME

The call to follow Jesus is a journey, a relationship; it is the fullness of life and how he leads us home.
—Ed Malone

MATTHEW, ONE OF THE ORIGINAL TWELVE DISCIPLES, began his gospel by giving the genealogy of Jesus, events surrounding his birth account, his baptism by John the Baptist, and Satan tempting him in the wilderness. Matthew reports that after John the Baptist was arrested, Jesus left the region around Jerusalem, moving north to the Sea of Galilee.

The scene Matthew describes next appears quite suddenly. He does not give enough information to fully understand the dynamic at play between Jesus and these fishermen:

> While walking by the Sea of Galilee, he saw two brothers, Simon (who is called Peter) and Andrew his brother, casting a net into the sea, for they were fishermen. And he said to them, "Follow me, and I will make you fishers of men." Immediately they left their nets and followed him. And going on from there he saw two other brothers, James the son of Zebedee and John his brother, in the boat with Zebedee their father, mending their nets, and he called them. Immediately they left the boat and their father and followed him. (Matt. 4:18–22)

Based on Matthew's report, we are left with questions. Did these fishermen make a spur-of-the-moment decision? Was Jesus exerting mind control over them? From all appearances, their response did not seem to be fully thought out. Any attempt to put myself into this exchange between Jesus and these fishermen was overwhelming.

Evaluating Appearances

Quite often, things are not as they appear. Many situations are not accurately assessed at first glance. Only when time is given to explore things more deeply can assumptions leading to the wrong conclusion be avoided.

One example of evaluating appearances is demonstrated when discovering that the sun does not move across the sky. What appears as the sun rising and setting is created by the movement of the earth. In fact, the earth rotates on its axis at a speed of 1,000 miles per hour while orbiting the sun at 66,000 miles per hour and is part of a solar system moving at 45,000 miles per hour. By all appearances, we are standing still, yet we are quite on the move!

We need to study all four Gospels as a combined record in order to answer the questions raised by Matthew's brief account. Each of the gospel writers records the life of Jesus with a particular emphasis in mind. John states that he did not write an exhaustive account of all Jesus did: "Now there are also many other things that Jesus did. Were every one of them to be written, I suppose that the world itself could not contain the books that would be written." "But these are written so that you may believe that Jesus is the Christ, the Son of God, and that by believing you may have life in his name" (John 21:25; 20:31).

What one gospel writer includes, others may leave out. John, writing thirty years after the other three, gives detailed information about the first four to six months of ministry Jesus had in the region around Jerusalem before going to Galilee. Additionally, John is the only one who gave a lengthy section of teaching on Spirit life at the Last Supper. Each gospel writer has unique material, and at the same time, parts of their story can be found in at least one or more of the other accounts.

Blending the writings of Matthew, Mark, Luke, and John is called a harmony of the Gospels. Both Mark and Matthew record the calling of these fishermen, while Luke and John do not. In that all four Gospels tell of the arrest of John the Baptist, a timeline point is established for arranging the early events in the ministry of Jesus. John has several chapters devoted to things Jesus did prior to going to Galilee.

Jesus submitted to John's baptism as an affirmation of John being the promised forerunner to the Messiah. John identified Jesus as the Lamb of God taking away the sins of the world, and he encouraged those around him to follow Jesus. Many of John's followers made the transition to Jesus, including Andrew and John, and in the days shortly afterward, Simon Peter, Philip, and Nathanael.

After Jesus's baptism and before the arrest of John the Baptist, Jesus cleansed the temple, chose disciples, met with Nicodemus, performed his first miracle at a wedding in Cana, attended Passover, and for a season conducted his ministry in parallel with John the Baptist. When John was taken into custody, Jesus moved north to the region around the Sea of Galilee.

The Full Story

By filling in Matthew's brief account with the material John gives, we have a better understanding of the call of these fishermen. John's gospel demonstrates that the calling by the sea was not their first encounter with Jesus. All but one of these fishermen are mentioned by name in John's gospel as already connected with Jesus. On that day by the sea, Jesus was asking them to take their commitment up a notch. Jesus was ready for them to devote all their time to the work at hand. They left their boats and followed.

This call of Jesus to follow him is difficult to transpose to a modern world. Imagine the response Jesus would get walking along Wall Street calling to executives, "Come, follow me." Even more pronounced, picture Jesus on the field at halftime during the Super Bowl calling to the players and fans. Jesus would be removed, and everyone's attention redirected to the center stage performance. Little consideration would be given to him, except for poking fun at and expressing disgust for the interruption of their party. Perhaps it is for the same reason Jesus made his call at the Sea of Galilee rather than the Colosseum in Rome. Calling fishermen rather than the religious leadership at the temple was also quite unexpected.

Many consider the call Jesus made to these fishermen as unique to the twelve disciples. Restricting the "Come, follow me" invitation to this inner group is not accurate. The gospel of Mark reports that Jesus gave this call to everyone: "And calling the crowd to him with his disciples, he said to them, 'If anyone would come after me, let him deny himself and take up his cross and follow me'" (Mark 8:34). This occasion of Jesus speaking to the crowd leaves no doubt that following him is a universal call.

These fishermen left everything to be with him, learn from him, and support him in the work he was doing. In order to stimulate your thinking about what it means to answer the call to follow Jesus, I offer the following allegory. By imagining the thoughts and experiences associated with the story, bridges leading to spiritual concepts can be generated. Word pictures are powerful in carrying a message. Jesus modeled this teaching technique throughout his ministry.

A Walk in the Woods

It was a normal spring day with the long-awaited budding of the trees, the grass turning green, and the smell of freshness in the air. It was a good day for a walk, and where better to walk than outdoors, away from the noise of the city? I was well underway when quite unexpectedly, at a fork in the trail, I encountered a fellow hiker.

He was a likable kind of guy with a love for and excitement about the wonders of nature. His invitation was quite unusual: "Come, follow me."

Startled by his request, I asked, "Where are you going?"

He responded with a childlike enthusiasm: "I'm going to hike the Appalachian Trail. Have you ever heard about it?"

His reply to my inquiry as to whether he had ever completed any portion of the Appalachian Trail was quite shocking: "No; how hard can it be? It is just a walk in the woods, right? We can figure it out as we go."

Considering that the AT stretches across fourteen states from Georgia to Maine for two thousand miles and takes the average hiker six to seven months to complete gave me confidence that the AT is not a fly-by-the-seat-of-your-pants adventure. Obviously, I declined his offer.

A Second Hiker

Expecting never to have such an encounter again, I resumed my hike. I was excited about walking in the depths of the woods, wading the creeks, and climbing the upcoming assent to an overlook, which promised a breathtaking view. With the sunlight dancing through the trees and the sights and sounds of nature all around, I settled back into my enthusiasm for what the trail offered. Not far up the path, a group of hikers was waiting as I crossed a footbridge spanning a small creek. The leader of the group said to me, "Come, go with us; we are training for the AT." This second hiker had completed the AT several times and was training others for their attempt at the trail. His offer to join their training regimen was certainly much more plausible to consider.

The Appeal of Jesus

In like fashion, Jesus stands at a fork in the trail of life we are traveling with the invitation, "Come, follow me." His call is made spiritually, pressing upon our inner self to follow him, by faith, on a different kind of journey. It is more than a walk in the woods. His approach to us is a larger-than-life experience filled with questions and even mystery. This is what Jesus might say to you:

> Come, follow me, I will take you home. There will be challenges requiring spiritual strength to get through. The journey is a process of change. The selfish part of you will

resist. Finding your way requires a shift in how you perceive things. Feeling and sensing your way spiritually will keep you on the right path. Trust me with this journey as it serves to transition you into the way of life at home.

Several things stand out from this allegory. For a project as big as the Appalachian Trail, one needs a trusted guide, training, and detailed, logistical planning. Successful hikers read stories and watch YouTube videos, absorbing the advice and heeding the warning given by veterans of the trail. Only 25 percent of those who start the AT complete the journey. It involves more than a walk in the woods.

Without question, Jesus is the only qualified guide to take us home. All that we need in order to complete the journey is available in the biblical record of his teachings and the continuing work of the Holy Spirit. Sadly, many professing followers of Jesus have no desire to listen to the instructions he gives about the journey we are to make with him. It is quite absurd that some folks spend more time equipping themselves to make a six-month hike than others do to complete their journey to our heavenly home.

Words Carefully Chosen

Following Jesus involves more than just believing something about the significance of his life. The expression "Follow me" sets the dynamic of an active, personal relationship as central to his invitation.

Some consider following Jesus as fulfilled by being a member of the local church. Participating in a body of believers is certainly a central principle of Christianity. However, what Jesus was asking involves more than who you spend time with on Sunday. We answer his call by imitating his life, living out his teaching, and yielding to his authority. It is a present, personal relationship of living life with him.

Many who identify themselves as Christians see no need to know what Jesus taught or how he lived. Asking professing Christians to identify at least five parables or important teachings Jesus gave, and further, to describe memorable events in his life they treasure and use to guide how they live, will be quite revealing. Pressing the same group to talk about living in a spiritual relationship with him may prove to be more than your audience can bear. However, in the same setting, mention something about their favorite sports team, music personality, or movie, and measure the difference in the depth, excitement, and content of the conversation. Regrettably, this situation applies to far too many people. Many think they can substitute simply believing something about Jesus for following him. They have no desire for anything more.

Empty Belief

I am certainly not alone in stating that many religious expressions within what is labeled as Christianity have produced empty-belief converts. Some think that if they believe Jesus lived and died on the cross for the forgiveness of sin, then all is well. Certainly, this statement is true and must be believed, but to do so does not fulfill what it means to follow Jesus. During his ministry, the demons were the first to acknowledge Jesus as the Holy One of God. They were certain of who Jesus was, but their belief did not save them.

"Come, follow me," is an active process. It is not a "been there, done that" kind of event. It is what you are doing right now. Following means moving to new places and participating in new experiences. By incorporating his teaching into our lives, we grow in our spiritual relationship of his living in us and through us. It is a supernatural way of life. There is much to learn involving change in who we are and how we live. Trusting his leading and following him closely brings fullness of life.

Paradigm Shift

It has been rightly stated that how you frame something makes a big difference. Recently, when I asked my dermatologist about a suspicious spot, the way she framed her answer caught my attention. She could have said: "A ship at sea, for as long as yours has been, will have barnacles on the hull; get used to it. The older you get, the more things you grow!" Instead, she put a nice frame around my concern by saying, "Your body produces these kinds of spots as you mature."

In art, the proper frame brings attention to the artwork; it influences how we see it, complements and completes it, and points to the heart of the piece of art. If frames have this kind of influence, the descriptor we use for salvation should point to the heart of how we view and respond to it.

For many, answering the call to follow Jesus is a strange way of framing the concept of salvation. Believing in Jesus to avoid hell and get in on heaven is the frame most are familiar with. The call to live in a spiritual relationship by following Jesus creates a different level of commitment; it is to join him in doing the will of the Father as a servant of the kingdom.

Translating the Greek word "faith" into the English word "believe" introduces the possibility of misunderstanding what Jesus intended. The English translation calling for us to believe in Jesus can have a shallow depth to it. For example, packing a lunch to go on a picnic because you believe it is not going to rain is not a deep level of commitment. However, the willingness to cross a footbridge spanning a cavern because you believe it is strong enough to carry your weight takes "believe" to a different level. Believing in Jesus without loving and following him can be nothing more than an intellectual acceptance of a fact.

Jesus called for everyone to follow him. It was the frame he felt best captured his intention for us. Whether we are living up to his call is easy to critique. When following someone, maintaining close contact is necessary. Knowing when the leader makes a radical shift in direction is critical. When the terrain becomes difficult to negotiate, the closer you stay to the leader allows you to take the best path to safety. There are times when matching the lead person's foot placement is the only way to stay safe and on the path.

Role Model

In sports, those learning the game usually adopt the style of a particular player. The mechanics of how a movement is executed, including even unique mannerisms of the role model, are adopted to achieve success. As a sports professional, it is an honor to have someone using your techniques. It involves more than wearing a shirt with your name and number on it. It is when the young player has perfected every aspect of your playing style. Imitation is truly the highest form of flattery.

What does it mean when professing Christians have no desire to follow Jesus as the model for living or to adopt his priority for doing the Father's will? Where do we stand in honoring Jesus? Wearing a cross as a piece of jewelry is not the same as living a "cross life."

There is a critical difference in believing in Jesus versus answering his call to follow him. Believing is much easier than following. Believing does not get in the way of how we live. The demons are a prime example. However, following him rips us away from our selfish and ungodly ways. When convinced that Jesus is the meaning of life, following him is not a have-to task. It is the desired opportunity to yield our lives to the one we admire, love, and want to be like. If we want to honor Jesus, we will want every detail of how he lived and what he taught to be manifested in our life. Jesus announced that few find the narrow gate to life. When we follow him as our guide, he will take us through the gate and along the path home.

A Word of Encouragement

Fishermen left their boats, sacrificing everything. Martyrs have followed Jesus even unto death. Many claiming to be Christians know nothing of his teachings or how he lived, or have any desire to live as he lived. Their focus is simply on what will happen to them when they die. There is but one standard for the proper response to our Lord as we allow him to live in us and be expressed through us. Following Jesus is a supernatural way of life for the few who are willing to pursue the path the crowd does not follow.

CHAPTER 2

DO YOU KNOW ME?

Scripture declares it a lie to say you know Jesus and abide in him when you do not follow his commands and live as he lived.
—Ed Malone

KNOWING JESUS IS MORE THAN BEING FAMILIAR WITH how he died. Abiding in him affects who you are and how you live. John, the author of the gospel and three epistles bearing his name, said, "And by this we know that we have come to know him, if we keep his commandments. Whoever says 'I know him' but does not keep his commandments is a liar, and the truth is not in him. . . . By this we may know that we are in him: whoever says he abides in him ought to walk in the same way in which he walked" (1 John 2:3–6).

It is important to notice the audience John addressed. He spoke of those who say they know Jesus and abide in him. Thinking that you do and saying you do doesn't make it true. Is it possible that the audience John addressed is still with us today?

The phrase "whoever says he abides in him ought to walk in the same way in which he walked" necessitates knowing how Jesus lived. Pursuing the question of how Jesus lived brings into focus pictures worth thousands of words. It is to look at his character, personality, and way of doing things. It is observing him embody the principles he taught.

When we know someone, there are several descriptive phrases we use to capture how they live as a reflection of who they are. Some people play a role, put on a good show, and try to impress others, but sooner or later their true character is demonstrated. Folks often express a variety of personality traits such as being stoic, bubbly, warm and fuzzy, serious-minded, laid-back, friendly, approachable, hard, harsh, sensitive, patient, giving, captivating, a thinker, often angry, emotionally expressive, and a good person, or one who lives by God-based priorities.

Based on your knowledge of Jesus, how would you describe him? What were his priorities in life? Do you know him or just know about him? The question of whether I knew Jesus was brought about by the following incident.

He Says He Is Jesus

Pastors are often called into unusual situations. One day I received a call from the police station concerning an individual detained for giving a false identity. "He says he's Jesus, and we need someone to make confirmation for us." When I told the officer that many people use the name Jesus, he said, "He says he is *Jesus*, the well-known one."

Based on Scripture, I was confident that the second coming of Jesus would be a bigger splash than an individual quietly walking the streets of our small town. On my way to the jail, I had some provoking thoughts. If there was not the conflict with Scripture, how would I know if this person was Jesus? Would I be able to sense a presence about him? Are there litmus-test questions that would guarantee his identity? If he could dazzle me with something touching upon the miraculous, would he win my approval?

Once at the police station, I was escorted to the holding cell. The individual looked to be in his twenties with long black hair, a beard, and was wearing a robe and sandals. When the cell door closed and the officer left, I was a bit startled. Being locked in a cell with an individual I believed to be unstable was a bit disconcerting.

The police officer who called was a personal friend and Christian brother concerned for a man needing help with issues bearing eternal consequences. My conversation with this Jesus impersonator was not very fruitful. However, I left this unusual experience thinking, *Do I know Jesus? As his follower, am I confident of his voice? Do I truly know Jesus or just know about him?*

The apostle John's concern for evidence that we know and abide in Jesus is a guard against having only a lip-service commitment. Jesus told those around him, and is telling us, that calling him Lord must be met with serving him as Lord through a heart connection, allowing us to know God and to be known by him. The intimacy of a relationship in knowing God runs throughout the New Testament:

"But if anyone loves God, he is known by God" (1 Cor. 8:3).

"But now that you have come to know God, or rather to be known by God . . ." (Gal. 4:9).

"The Lord knows those who are his" (2 Tim. 2:19).

"I am the good shepherd. I know my own and my own know me" (John 10:14).

Knowing and abiding in Jesus, evidenced by following his commands and living as he lived, is not a hard expectation for those who love him. It is the decision they made when choosing to follow him: to walk and live as Jesus requires, absorbing the story of his life. The Gospels record numerous occasions of Jesus interacting with others. Observing how he expressed his love is instructive and inspiring.

To Jerusalem

Approaching the final week of his ministry, Jesus crossed the Jordan River and entered the city of Jericho. His destination was Jerusalem. Because Joshua had left the wilderness and had led Israel across the Jordan into Jericho, the crowd stepped up their enthusiasm when Jesus entered Jericho by the same path. The biblical account of the trip Jesus made to Jerusalem is brief. The significance of what happened along the way can be easily overlooked.

Jesus led the way, but not to the goal the crowd anticipated. There was agony in his soul as he walked. The people were still confused and misdirected. Even the disciples were not prepared for what would happen. The days ahead would be emotionally intense, spiritually draining, and physically painful. There was much Jesus wanted to do to ease the blow of what those around him were unwilling to accept as his mission. Obviously, a host of thoughts swirled through his head.

During the excitement, a blind man, sitting by the roadside and hearing Jesus's voice, began crying out to Jesus. He was rebuked and told to be silent by some of the crowd. Their sentiment was that Jesus had more important things to do. They were wrong—Jesus stopped.

It would have been understandable to excuse Jesus for not hearing the call of the blind man or for asking the blind man to wait for a more reasonable time. After all, eternal issues were at stake as Jesus approached Jerusalem. But in the chaos, Jesus stopped. Not only was he sensitive to hear, but he was caring enough not to walk by. Asking ourselves how we would have responded in a similarly pressurized situation can be quite revealing. Jesus set the bar high for those committed to walking as he walked.

The question Jesus posed to the blind man seemed unnecessary: "What do you want me to do for you?" "Master, let me receive my sight" was his response. At that moment, Jesus wanted the crowd to acknowledge their blindness as Bartimaeus did. If so, he could help them see that their desires were temporal and his eternal. Also, they would be able to see that what they wanted was centered in the things of the flesh, whereas his desire was centered in the soul; yet they believed they saw clearly. Like us, they had no problem seeing what they wanted.

As Jesus continued through Jericho, the noise and excitement of the crowd picked up. Praise unto God was still being announced as a result of healing Bartimaeus. Once again, Jesus is not focused on himself, but senses that someone is desperate to see him. Jesus stopped, looked up into a tree, and called for Zacchaeus, the tax collector, to come down that he might dine with him.

The crowd was excited when they crossed the Jordan, and now, with the healing of Bartimaeus, their enthusiasm was ramped up even more. This is not a time to stop. It is a time to strike while the iron is hot. Not so with Jesus; he is not motivated by the frenzy of a crowd.

DO YOU KNOW ME?

Zacchaeus, being a tax collector, represented all that was offensive to the Jews. For many, this stop was too much, and they left disgusted. The ability of Jesus not to be blinded by prejudice and self-focus allowed an individual to enter the kingdom. Remaining spiritually sensitive in distracting circumstances demonstrated an admirable quality of how Jesus lived.

Approach to the City

After the healing of Bartimaeus and the stop for Zacchaeus, the twenty-mile journey to Jerusalem resumed. The well-known caravan route was a winding path, with olive trees terracing the steep hillsides. The nature of the terrain made it easy for robbers to attack. It was a mountain hike comprising seventeen hundred feet of elevation change from Jericho to Jerusalem. Folks from Bethany and Bethphage joined the group. Additionally, more people came from Jerusalem to join his entry into their capital city.

At one point, there is a ridge that provides a view of the lower city of Jerusalem. With this first glance of the city, excitement escalated, knowing that soon they would reach their destination. As they continued, the city goes out of view. The next part of the trip presents a rugged upward ascent that leads to a smooth rock ledge. The view is breathtaking. The entire city, including the temple, was displayed like a painting no artist could capture. Excitement filled the air with explosive enthusiasm as shouts of "Hosanna" began. The euphoria of the crowd was reaching peak expression. Fueled by confusion and misdirection, the scene approached pandemonium. Then the strangest thing happened. Once again, Jesus stops.

Agony of Heart

Overlooking the city, he wept. God in the flesh was overwhelmed with emotion. The word used here is not the same as when Jesus wept at the tomb of Lazarus—a quiet weeping at the grave of his friend. When Jesus saw the city, it was a loud, deep lamentation. The agony of his heart was not soothed by the excitement of the crowd. He wept not for himself or what awaited him, but for those who rejected his offer of life. His words are penetrating: "Would that you, even you, had known on this day the things that make for peace! But now they are hidden from your eyes . . . because you did not know the time of your visitation" (Luke 19:42, 44).

Peace (shalom) was the most desired state of being among the Jews. "Shalom" was the prayer of greeting that Jews exchanged with each other. Peace with God (especially in a covenant relationship), peace with others, and a peace surpassing understanding were desired by all. It is generated by what is going on inside of us rather than being dependent on what is happening on the outside. Isaiah says, "The way of peace they do not know, and there is no justice in their paths; they have made their roads crooked; no one who treads on them knows peace" (Isa. 59:8).

It is hard to imagine that those who were considered to be the people of God did not know Jesus. What they pursued through their religion left them unable to recognize God in the flesh. Israel attended meetings, sang songs, and recited prayers without a heart connection with God. Many in our day function in the same way. The great evangelist and missionary Charles Wesley is often credited with the statement, "Professing Christians have just enough religion to make them miserable."

Many embrace Christianity with a superficial commitment. Observing religion as a set of beliefs and rituals is empty. Wesley's statement of just enough religion to make them miserable indicates some, but not a wholehearted commitment. As a result, professing Christians are not happy in the world and are not fulfilled in their faith. They are trapped because they cannot do what they want, and they don't desire what they should. They are troubled by guilt, fear, and uncertainty, producing a miserable existence.

The dividing point between being religious and finding peace with God is the difference between intellectual acceptance of concepts and having a relationship with him. It is to be changed by his Spirit, to follow him as Shepherd, and to love him more than life. It is to see God as supreme in value and to allow him to be supreme in authority. Religion is simply outward conformity to rules and rituals. Relationship with God is a matter of a change in our hearts, which transforms who we are and how we live. It is the difference of a few rather than many being saved.

The scary part of enough religion to be miserable makes one doubly lost. Professing Christians think they are in a relationship with God, but they are not. In this state, it is hard to give them what they think they have. Such was the situation Jesus faced with the crowd around him. In less than a week, the shouts of "Hosanna!" would become "Crucify him!"

Jesus wept when he looked upon Jerusalem. Israel's religion and attachment to their traditions made them blind to him. The contrast between the agony Jesus felt while looking at the city and the excitement of the crowd was huge. Jesus cared deeply. He could have just enjoyed the moment of misplaced praise, but that was not possible. Jesus entered the city with tears while the crowd entered with cheers. Once again, Jesus startles us with this stop as he expressed the depth of his desire to give Israel the peace they needed. As his followers, are the things of God important enough to us to make us cry? As his followers, living as he lived means feeling what he felt.

The Last Week

This last week of ministry in Jerusalem was full of intensity. The cleansing of the temple and the parable of the vineyard created confusion among the once-excited crowd. Teachings such as to render unto Caesar that which belongs to Caesar pushed even more out of favor with him. In the heat of conflict, Jesus maintained an exemplary presence of patience and peace. We need to learn how to live as he lived when the pressure is on.

On the evening before the crucifixion, Jesus observed the annual celebration of Passover with his disciples. They moved from the upper room to a garden place of prayer. With all his heart, Jesus prayed, "Not as I will, but as you will." He had the opportunity to lay his life down or pick it up. Followers of Jesus understand that the will of the Father is the guiding principle of life, regardless of whether it is easy, hard, painful, or pleasant.

In the darkness of that night, the light of torches was seen and the voices of those who approached were heard. Armed, battle-hardened soldiers were among those in that mob. Their mission was to take Jesus by whatever means were required.

Jesus knew that the disciples were not prepared for what was about to take place and that the situation could get out of control. He would not die on this night, nor would he allow his disciples to die in this garden. He would die at the proper time by the will of the Father, not by the hands of a mob.

The scene developed quickly. Weapons were in readiness for a fight. Jesus took the initiative and assured the mob that he would not resist. Even so, Peter swung his sword, striking the person closest to him. The spark was ignited. The battle was on. Quickly, Jesus quieted the storm as he did in a boat on the Sea of Galilee. Jesus assured the mob that their objective had been achieved. He yielded without a fight. Peter was bewildered, considering he had put his life on the line for Jesus. The rest of the disciples were confused and afraid. The arresting mob was relieved that the fight was over and surprised that Jesus gave up willingly.

Jesus Stops Again

Confusion and intense emotions filled the air as they prepared to descend from this hillside place of prayer. Then once again, Jesus stopped. Everyone grew tense. Had he changed his mind? The soldiers quickly took their stance. What happened took everyone by surprise. What is revealed about Jesus humbles all who seek to live as he lived.

The one struck by Peter's sword was a servant of Malchus the priest. One would assume that he was not there by choice. Possibly, he was commissioned to carry the torch so that the others would have their hands free. This task would have placed him at the front and the closest to Peter. This unnamed servant struck by Peter's sword was a concern for Jesus.

All eyes were fixed on Jesus as he moved toward the servant, who possibly knelt in pain, holding his wound to suppress the bleeding. Compassionately, Jesus healed the wound. No words were spoken. As Jesus looked into the eyes of this frightened and hurting servant, love flowed.

Jesus rejoined the arresting entourage. They bound him and took him to the authorities. I can imagine that the walk back to the city was made in silence. What could anyone say? Jesus had yielded without a fight. They had witnessed a healing. More than that, they were given a glimpse into the heart of God. This scene of how Jesus lived makes using the word *Christian* (Christlike) to describe who we are quite a stretch.

Who is this man that the wind and sea obey him and angry mobs are quieted by him? Who is this who stopped to heal a blind man, to eat with a sinner, to weep over a city, and to heal the ear of one who was part of an arresting mob?

Jesus has no equal. Who would have thought about the one struck by Peter's sword? Jesus did. This servant was innocent. He was simply carrying out the will of his master. He did not deserve the brunt of Peter's sword. Jesus rights the wrong inflicted upon this man. The parallels between this servant and Jesus stand out boldly.

God on Trial

In the early hours of Friday morning, long before dawn, Jesus was taken before Annas, the previous high priest. From there he appeared before Caiaphas, the current high priest. Next, he was set before the Sanhedrin, and then was sent on to Pilate who asked that Herod Antipas, who had jurisdiction over Galilee, hear the case. Jesus was sent back to Pilate where he was mocked, beaten, and sent to Golgotha for crucifixion. The absurdity of God on trial and the injustice of having done nothing wrong was met by Jesus with calm composure. Our being in the same situation probably would not yield the same response.

Jesus endured the pain of the cross for several hours. It is one of the most agonizing ways to die, aptly described as death by suffocation with unbearable pain. While on the cross suffering the pain and listening to the scoffers, Jesus stopped once again. Instead of focusing on himself and the injustice that was inflicted upon him, he loved to the end. His thoughts are not what one would have expected. When it was difficult even to breathe, he was heard praying: "Father, forgive them, for they know not what they do." And later, he had the sensitivity to say to the disciple standing by, "Behold, your mother!" At his most challenging moment in the flesh, he held back the pain long enough to use what little air he was getting into his lungs to make sure Mary was cared for. Jesus never ceases to amaze those who choose to follow him.

The interval between the resurrection and ascension continued to reveal the depth of Jesus's character. The patience he displayed with Thomas, who struggled to believe, and the time he took with Peter to lovingly restore their relationship continued to reveal who he was and how he lived.

At the Beginning

The way Jesus lived out this last week of ministry was quite revealing. Without a doubt, Jesus finished his journey well. How he lived during the early years of his life, before starting his public ministry with baptism by John the Baptist, is an appropriate question. The first miracle in Cana provides a glimpse into his earlier years:

> On the third day there was a wedding at Cana in Galilee, and the mother of Jesus was there. Jesus also was invited to the wedding with his disciples. When the wine ran out, the mother of Jesus said to him, "They have no wine." And Jesus said to her, "Woman, what does this have to do with me? My hour has not yet come." His mother said to the servants, "Do whatever he tells you." (John 2:1–5)

At first thought, addressing Mary as "woman" is a bit troubling. Nothing in the text indicates that Mary was bothered by the comment.

When on the cross, Jesus says to her, "Woman, behold, your son!" (John 19:26). Culturally, it was a polite way to address a lady.

The brief conversation between Jesus and Mary at the wedding reveals what Mary's experience with her son had been like during the last thirty years. Mary tells Jesus that the family has a need. Running out of wine would have been an embarrassment. The response Jesus gives to her is quite unusual. I would guess this was not the first time Jesus said something hard for his mother to understand. For Mary, one thing was certain: let Jesus know about the need, and it will be taken care of. Her mission was accomplished. Without any further discussion, Mary turns to the servants and says, "Do whatever he tells you."

The confidence to walk away without an absolute answer is a credit to the character of Jesus. With certainty, Mary knows he will meet the need, and she tells the servants to do whatever he said. Followers of Jesus should be counted on in the same way. Most people would have said: "This is not my problem; go talk to someone else."

The response of the servants to Mary's instruction to do whatever Jesus says is impressive. Jesus told them to fill the pots with water used for ceremonial cleansing. Scripture says there were six stone jars holding thirty gallons each, and they filled them to the brim. Tell a teenager to fill the pots and see what you get. As followers of Jesus, we should have the reputation of being counted on to help, doing whatever he says, and like the servants, doing what he says to the brim!

Who Touched Me?

Another example of how Jesus lived is recorded in the fifth chapter of Mark, and it's one that has always impressed me. At this time, Jesus was doing a lot of miracles. Crowds flocked to him wherever he went. On this occasion, Jesus was by the Sea of Galilee, and a great multitude surrounded him. A ruler of the synagogue asked Jesus to go to his house and heal his daughter. The crowd went with Jesus to the house of Jairus. As they walked, Jesus stopped and asked, "Who touched me?" The disciples are beside themselves, telling Jesus that there are people crowding all around. Jesus told them that this was more than physical contact.

A woman with a bleeding problem had approached Jesus in the crowd, seeking to touch him, believing it would be enough for the healing she had sought for twelve years. In response to her faith, she was healed and had slipped off into the crowd. Jesus stopped and looked for her. She came trembling in fear and knelt at his feet.

The religious sentiment was that she was ritually unclean due to her bleeding problem. Now that she had touched Jesus, she had made him unclean as well. She was fearful of how Jesus would react. This is an occasion where Jesus could have healed her and continued to the house of Jairus. Instead, Jesus stopped so that she could have much more.

Jesus wanted her to know that he did not share the view of the religious establishment that she was unclean. As she knelt at his feet, Jesus addressed her as daughter and told her to go in peace. Taking the time to give her more than she was seeking and letting her know that the people's view of her being unclean was not how God felt was to liberate her to full healing. She hadn't stolen her healing, but had received it through faith as a gift from God. The way Jesus spoke to this woman trembling at his feet warms my heart. Tenderly, he told her that she was not an outcast, but rather was a daughter. The powerful touch of spirits between Jesus and the woman was special. Touching Jesus's robe was a simple thing to do, yet it was life-changing for her and it was challenging to the misdirected thinking of the crowd to witness it.

A New Look

As a follower of Jesus, reading the Gospels to observe how he lived takes the Scriptures to a new level. Watching him live by the principles he taught is golden. Learning how he lived is like sitting in front of a piece of artwork and observing the finer details that often go unnoticed.

Our goal is to be familiar with the events in his life in such a way that the words on the page become pictures. By placing ourselves in the crowd or even as the central figure in what is happening, we enlarge our understanding of Jesus. By this approach, reading the Gospels will be like turning the pages of a picture album. Pictures take us back to a place full of sights, smells, sounds, and emotions. A picture truly is a thousand words capturing a moment in time. It is important not only to know what Jesus said, but also to know how he lived. The Gospels provide a lot of pictures to enjoy.

If the test of whether I know Jesus is expressed in living as he did, how do I measure up? Do I know him or just know about him? Do I love him, abide in him, and follow his commands? Do I just want to use him to get to heaven, or do I follow him as he is the source of life? Could I recognize Jesus in a crowd? What would guarantee his identity to me? Knowing Jesus by following him is vastly different than knowing about him. The standard of Scripture is high for how we should live. If you know him, you will follow his commands. If you abide in him, you will live as he lived. All who love and admire him reach for this.

A Word of Encouragement

To walk as he walked is a tall order. Followers of Jesus know that even with his indwelling power, our lives will pale in comparison to his. Striving to live as he lived still remains the goal and allows him to carry us to heights unattainable on our own.

CHAPTER 3

Enormous Task

The physical pain Jesus endured on the cross was undeniable. On the other hand, the emotional and spiritual battle he experienced throughout his ministry often goes unnoticed. In his effort to deliver his people from their man-made religious traditions, conflict arose, costing him his life.
—Ed Malone

MOST PEOPLE, EVEN THOSE IN CHURCH FAIL TO APPRECI-ate the struggle Jesus faced in his ministry. Exposure to random pieces of his teaching and miracles fails to capture what life was like for him on a daily basis. The hostility against Jesus was extreme. The confusion in his audience based on their lack of true knowledge of God created enormous issues. The complexities of the Jewish faith based on their traditions made for emotional responses to his call for change. It is true that the Jews wanted a Davidic type of king to lead them to peace and prosperity. However, it was the challenge Jesus made to their religious system that provoked their leadership's call for his life.

The crowds attracted to Jesus gave the appearance that the whole world was willing to follow him, yet their motivation was in the wrong place. Their focus was on the benefits of his miracle-working power. For example, after feeding the five thousand, the crowds came to Capernaum looking for Jesus. Jesus confronted those coming back for another mira-cle: "Truly, truly, I say to you, you are seeking me, not because you saw signs, but because you ate your fill of the loaves" (John 6:26).

As followers of Jesus, we need to know more than a few of his sayings or miracles he performed. We must embrace all he stood for in confronting the religious expression of his day. We need to appreciate the struggle he endured as he lived out the Father's will.

Jesus was clear when challenging the Jewish form of religion. He identified their doctrines as rules made by men. He cleansed the temple, calling it a den of thieves. He rejected their ceremonial cleansing of pots and pans as outward rather than inward renewal. His healing on the Sabbath sparked a call to battle. His mission of giving the people what they needed clashed with their desire for him to give them what they wanted. Conflict erupted and emotions raged when Jesus offered what they believed they already had—true knowledge of and relationship with God.

Prophet, Priest, King

In the role of a prophet, Jesus called for change. The repentance movement initiated by John the Baptist was the foundation upon which Jesus launched his mission. His message was confronting because he spoke truth. Truth confronts because it exposes sin.

As priest, Jesus fulfilled the sacrificial system instituted by Moses. In his death, he became the once-for-all sacrifice for sin. By his sacrifice, the Jewish system of law-keeping salvation was replaced by grace through faith. Jesus opened the inner sanctuary of the temple to all followers, regardless of ethnicity, gender, or special status as a priest. He called for an inclusive gospel embracing tax collectors, sinners, and Gentiles. For most of his Jewish brethren, it was too much to ask.

As king, Jesus established his rule. When challenged by Pilate, Jesus spoke of his kingdom being in the world, but not of the world. His kingdom had no geographical boundaries, armies, or a ruling race. It is a kingdom where God's will is done on earth as it is in heaven.

Messiah, Teacher, Moral Guide

As Messiah, Jesus came as promised. He cleansed lepers, healed the sick, raised the dead, and preached good news to the poor. Miracles were performed as acts of compassion and authentication of him as Messiah. His miracle ministry proved to be a huge distraction. The people selfishly wanted the personal benefits of the miracle rather than allowing the miracle to be a sign pointing them to the one they should follow.

As teacher, Jesus taught with a depth that reached the soul. His teaching pointed to inward principles affecting outward behavior. The centrality of loving God and others was held as the highest objective. Truly, no one taught as Jesus with wisdom, authority, and the words of life.

As a moral guide, Jesus set the highest standard throughout his life and his teaching. Yet when it came to convincing the people that they were spiritually blind, he was not received.

Fellow Traveler

As a fellow traveler in life, Jesus understood the struggle of the soul. Those rejecting him became forever alienated from the Father. It was difficult for many to find the spiritual strength necessary to listen to his message. Within family groups, some followed, and others didn't. Overcoming the struggle of the soul to follow Jesus without feeling as if they were spitting on their fathers' graves was hard for most to overcome. Blinded by a form of religion and committed more to ethnic traditions than pursuit of God left many unable to listen to Jesus.

The task in front of Jesus would have been easier had he been the type of person who does what needs to be done, letting the chips fall where they may with a like-it-or-lump-it attitude. But he wasn't. As mentioned in the previous chapter, Jesus looked over Jerusalem and wept. Their rejection hurt. It pierced his soul when they refused his offer of life. The people were spiritually blind and did not know God when they thought they did. He accepted their unwillingness to follow him—even when it tore at his heart.

Even with Jesus possessing all wisdom and fullness of the Spirit, he was able to rescue only a few from their lack of true relationship with the Father. Since they did not have a heart connection with God, they were unwilling to receive his words. Convinced that they already had what they needed, their ability to respond to him was blocked. An overview of his three-year ministry reveals an increasing resistance to his message by those who should have embraced him, and it gives us the opportunity to be in touch with what life was like for him.

Public Ministry

Jesus started his ministry in the region of Judea, lasting about six months. The cleansing of the temple and Sabbath healings created conflict with the religious leadership. After the arrest of John the Baptist, Jesus went to the region around the Sea of Galilee.

While in Galilee, Jesus traveled from town to town for eighteen months, ramping up his miracle ministry. As a result, crowds came out as news of him reached their town. At this point, it appears as if everyone is ready to follow this new teacher. However, meetings in the synagogues were occasions of intense debate, resulting in Jesus being called demon-possessed. The crowds were primarily focused on the personal benefits of his miracles, while the religious leadership wanted him dead. Even those in his hometown of Nazareth tried to kill him. Confusion, misplaced allegiance, and hatred swirled around Jesus. It was only when he retreated to the countryside that great teaching sessions like the Sermon on the Mount were given.

Time of Withdrawal

During the next six months, Jesus withdrew to towns away from the land of Israel. He was just one year from the crucifixion. During this time, he worked directly with the twelve disciples. There was much to learn, and time was running out. They went to places such as Tyre, Sidon, Phoenicia, the Decapolis, and Bethsaida. There was one brief visit to Dalmanutha (Magdala) in Galilee, only to reveal that the opposition against him had not subsided. In fact, rival parties of the Pharisees and the Sadducees were willing to join forces in attacking him.

Jesus withdrew to Bethsaida, and then went to Caesarea Philippi. As the feeding of the five thousand was a pivotal point with the miracle-seeking crowds, so now Jesus reached a pivotal point with the twelve. After feeding the five thousand, Jesus turned the miracle-seeking crowds away on their return the next day. It was now time for his disciples to accept his role as redeemer Messiah.

Who Am I?

When Jesus asked the disciples about the perception of the people concerning his identity, there were varied responses: "'Some say John the Baptist, others say Elijah, and others Jeremiah or one of the prophets.' He said to them, 'But who do you say that I am?' Simon Peter replied, 'You are the Christ, the Son of the living God'" (Matt. 16:14–16).

Peter had the right answer. How he arrived at this conclusion was important. Was it when he met Jesus walking on the water that he knew, or was it when he saw Jesus raise the dead, heal the sick, and cast out demons? Maybe it was when Jesus fearlessly faced the death threats hurled at him or the challenges of the religious leaders questioning his understanding of God. Certainly, the teaching of Jesus calling for change struck a chord at the core of Peter's heart. In his alliance with John the Baptist, Peter was already convinced that change was needed.

Spiritual Decision

Jesus summed up the key to Peter's understanding of him: "Blessed are you, Simon Bar-Jonah! For flesh and blood has not revealed this to you, but my Father who is in heaven" (Matt. 16:17). Peter's announcement of Jesus as the Messiah was made through his spiritual relationship with the Father. However, Peter's view of what it meant for Jesus to be the Messiah was wrong.

Jesus explained to his disciples that he must go to Jerusalem and suffer many things at the hands of the elders, chief priests, and teachers of the law. He told them that he would be killed and on the third day would be raised to life. Peter took him aside and began to rebuke him:

"Far be it from you, Lord! This shall never happen to you." Jesus turned and said to Peter, "Get behind me, Satan! You are a hindrance to me. For you are not setting your mind on the things of God, but on the things of man" (Matt. 16:22–23).

To be so right and then so wrong, to be taught by God and then to resort to the things of men is a huge shift. Peter was like the blind man in Bethsaida whom Jesus healed before coming to Caesarea Philippi. In this healing, Jesus touched the blind man and asked him what he saw: "I see people, but they look like trees, walking" (Mark 8:24).

After touching him the second time, the blind man saw things clearly. As with the blind man, Peter needs continuing touches of the Master before he sees things clearly. Peter saw some truth, but not all of the truth. Even to the final week, when Jesus was in Gethsemane, Peter swung his sword to protect his Master. Embracing a Messiah who would atone for sin through his death was hard to accept. Like Peter, many hear from God at one point and then put a man-made spin on it. How tiring it must have been for Jesus to deal with misconceptions about who he was, even among his closest followers. It seemed as if everywhere he turned, preconceived, man-made concepts presented a challenge to the truth he presented.

For Jesus, his ministry wasn't a walk in the park. Emotions, debate, anger, repeated attempts to kill him, confusion, and selfish interests created a battlefield difficult to negotiate. His task was tiring, emotionally draining, and spiritually intense as he wrestled with those convinced they were walking in the truth of God.

Back South

After spending six months outside of Israel, Jesus traveled south to regions around Jerusalem. He worked in the territories of Judea and Perea, which lay east and west of the Jordan River. Six months remained before the crucifixion.

Jesus spent three months in Judea, where he had begun his public ministry alongside John the Baptist. John 7–10 and Luke 10–13 give details of that time period. The question among the people now reached an open debate about Jesus being the Messiah. For the people to raise such a suggestion caused a feeding frenzy among the religious leaders. Jesus spoke of being the light of the world, and he confronted those around him as having the devil as their father. They attempted to stone him, but Jesus left unharmed.

The healing of a man born blind stirred the authorities to almost uncontrollable anger. This was a miracle hard to deny. The announcement by Jesus of being the Good Shepherd in the vein of Ezekiel's promise was more than the rulers could stand. At the Feast of Dedication, which ends his time in Judea, Jesus does not openly answer the question of being the Messiah, and the Jewish leadership attempted once again to stone him for blasphemy—calling himself the Son of God and thereby making himself God (John 10:33).

Messiah?

The issue of Jesus openly declaring that he was the Messiah produced a lot of questions. To say that he was the Messiah among those who have a political revolution in mind would have communicated the wrong message. Throughout the Galilean tours when the demons announced who Jesus was, they were silenced. If Jesus accepted the title of Messiah too early, the Jewish leadership could have easily persuaded Rome to get rid of him.

During the early Judean period, John the Baptist announced Jesus as the Lamb of God who takes away the sins of the world. Also, during this same time, Philip went to Peter and said that they had found the Messiah. However, Jesus being the Messiah went silent until Peter's confession at Caesarea Philippi. Even then, at that late stage of ministry, his disciples were unwilling to accept that it meant for him to die.

During the last three months before the crucifixion, Jesus spent time in Bethany beyond the Jordan. During that time, Jesus dined with sinners, healed on the Sabbath, and taught those around him to count the cost of following him. Time was running out for Israel to awaken to her Messiah. Passover loomed on the horizon. Close by Jerusalem, in the city of Bethany, Jesus raised Lazarus from the dead, and his fate with the religious leadership was sealed. They knew that if they did not act quickly, things would move beyond their control.

Final Week

The final entry of Jesus into Jerusalem is recorded in Matthew 21, Mark 11, Luke 19, and John 12. All four Gospels contribute to the details of this final week. The crowds were pressing for a political Messiah, and the religious leaders wanted Jesus dead. When Jesus cursed the barren fig tree, cleansed the temple for the second time, and told the parable of the vineyard, it was clear that the end was near. Debates arose about paying taxes, the greatest commandment, and the resurrection of the dead, which the leadership tried to use in building a case of blasphemy against him.

In a whirlwind tour, we have sketched the ministry of Jesus. We have only hit the high points. The goal is to help you understand the dynamic of those three years. The task Jesus faced was complex, emotionally charged, and steeped in conflict. Most of the Jews had a misplaced allegiance to their ethnic religion instead of to God. Getting a glimpse of Jesus living in the conflict of our world is essential for us in following him.

A Fellow Pilgrim

The writer of Hebrews emphasizes that Jesus is a faithful priest over us because he entered our situation: "Therefore he had to be made like his brothers in every respect, so that he might become a merciful and faithful high priest in the service of God" (Heb. 2:17).

This brief outline of his ministry reveals the road Jesus walked as being extremely difficult. Crowds clamored after him with selfish motives, and more than once the protective hand of the Father intervened to spare his life. Even the twelve failed to comprehend how his mission was to unfold. He stood toe-to-toe with the devil's assault. He cared deeply, bringing him much pain of heart. His life among us was not a paradise retreat, but a battlefield. He fought the good fight of the faith. He navigated life well, meeting the challenges thrown at him without sacrificing his mission or his sinlessness. The beauty of his life was expressed in how he lived and what he gave so that we might live.

He is the one who leads because he is the only one qualified for the position. He is a veteran of the trail, having weathered the storms of life. Learn from him, stay close to him, and enjoy the experience of him living in you and being expressed through you. Absorb everything recorded in the Scriptures as you walk through life with him.

Part of knowing someone is to understand what that person is passionate about. Until you are in touch with the driving force of someone's life, you don't really know them. Jesus displayed an overriding passion to bring glory to and live out the Father's will. His willingness to be a servant meeting the needs of others colored all that he did. There were principles in life he deemed worth dying for. In the next chapter, we will look more closely at Jesus taking his stand against the abuse of the temple and their observance of the Sabbath. As his followers, we must grasp why these issues were so important. How can you admire, love, and follow someone unless you appreciate and agree with the things that drive their life?

In the previous chapter, we asked who this man was whom the wind and sea obey and who can quiet angry mobs. Who is this who stopped to heal a blind man, to eat with a sinner, to weep over Jerusalem, and to heal the ear of one who was part of an arresting mob?

We continue by asking who this is who emptied himself of his godly privileges to pitch his tent among us. He is the one by whom and for whom all things were created, who not only emptied himself, but also became a servant. In doing so, he was looking not to his own interests, but to ours. Not only was he willing to accept mistreatment, but he was also willing to accept death by crucifixion. Jesus set no boundaries for how far he would go in accomplishing the will of the Father. The emotional and physical abuse, cruel mocking, being treated with contempt, being considered as demon-possessed, and repeated attempts to kill him while securing life for others would be for us too much to bear.

Jesus faced an enormous task in living among us. He gave himself completely for the needs of others. He was under no mandate except the press of love. It certainly makes the call for us to live as he lived quite the undertaking. The term Christian (Christlike) was coined by those outside of the faith to describe followers of Jesus. To be Christlike is first and foremost to be a servant.

In chapter 2, we looked at the sensitivity and response of love Jesus demonstrated in his daily living. This chapter has focused on the extent to which he gave up his godly privileges and how far he went to serve the will of the Father. As his followers, we are called to do the same. Many have followed his lead and others continue daily to follow his lead in standing against the evil of the world. What he endured to make it possible for us to connect with him is a level of love beyond compare.

A Word of Encouragement

There was nothing easy about the mission Jesus accomplished. Even so, compelled by love and devoted to truth, he came to give us life and set us free from sin and man-made religious traditions. To love as he loved and serve as he served is the mission of his followers.

CHAPTER 4

HILL WORTH DYING ON

Jesus took his stand on a hill worth dying on when he cleansed the temple and healed on the Sabbath. These two pillars of the Jewish faith, meant to be a means of connecting the people with God, had acquired a misplaced focus.
—Ed Malone

WHEN JESUS WAS IN JUDEA BEFORE THE ARREST OF JOHN the Baptist, he caused quite a stir: "In the temple he found those who were selling oxen and sheep and pigeons, and the money-changers sitting there. And making a whip of cords, he drove them all out of the temple, with the sheep and oxen. And he poured out the coins of the money-changers and overturned their tables. And he told those who sold pigeons, 'Take these things away; do not make my Father's house a house of trade'" (John 2:14–16).

Animals running in all directions, people trying to get out of the way, tables overturned, and coins spread across the ground sent a shockwave of chaos throughout the temple. Why did Jesus take such a forceful step? What was so important that he risked his life to address?

Jerusalem was the nation's capital, and the temple located there was the central focus of all things Jewish. Solomon built the first temple on land purchased by David, replacing the tabernacle of Moses. "Touch this sacred place of worship and die" was known by all who visited their city.

Within the temple, a warning was displayed instructing Gentiles not to move beyond the barrier of the outer court. Specifically, no foreigner was to enter within the forecourt or the balustrade around the sanctuary. Whoever was caught would have himself to blame for his subsequent death. An example of the enforcement of this is found in Acts 21. Paul was accused of bringing a Greek into the restricted area of the temple. He was dragged out and was being beaten when a cohort of Roman soldiers intervened to save his life. It was no small thing for Jesus to cleanse the temple.

The focus at the temple had evolved into something far removed from God's intention. The common expression of missing the point certainly applies to why Jesus cleansed the temple. Tragically, like the cultures around them, Israel looked upon their sacrificial system as the way to please God. The sacrifices that were intended to impress the seriousness of sin and cause a change in how Israel lived no longer had that effect. The temple, meant to be a means of connecting people with God as a house of prayer, had become a noisy and distracting marketplace.

The buying and selling activities were conducted in the court of the Gentiles. In this part of the temple, non-Jews came as seekers of God. These moneymaking transactions were a barrier rather than a means for Gentiles to know God.

From across the nation, Jewish males traveled to Jerusalem to observe three required annual feast days (celebrations). The expense of being on the road, fees paid to convert their money to temple money, exorbitant prices charged for sacrificial animals, and a temple tax made these gatherings costly. Elaborate rituals, professional music, and the detailed ornamentation of the building made for a festive gathering. However, supporting all of this was a heavy burden carried on the backs of the poor.

God did not want his people strapped with this cost. He did not live in the house (overlaid with gold) they had built for him. Sadly, folks left these celebrations with empty pockets to make a tiring journey home, feeling they had fulfilled God's desire. Pomp, ceremony, and good entertainment in plush surroundings were not why God wanted his people to gather.

Old Testament Issue as Well

The problem Jesus confronted concerning the temple was not something new. In Amos 5, Hosea 6, Isaiah 1, and Micah 6, these prophets spoke for God in a unified voice saying, "I hate, I despise your feasts; take away the noise of your songs. I desire mercy, not sacrifice; even though you make many prayers, I will not listen." The message of these prophets was for God's people to be just with others, live according to God's standard of righteousness, cease to do evil, learn to do good, love kindness, and walk humbly with him.

The psalmist writes:

Not for your sacrifices do I rebuke you; your burnt offerings are continually before me.

If I were hungry, I would not tell you, for the world and its fullness are mine. Do I eat the flesh of bulls or drink the blood of goats?

The one who offers thanksgiving as his sacrifice glorifies me; to one who orders his way rightly I will show the salvation of God! (Ps. 50:8, 12–13, 23)

If temple observance doesn't confront the people with God, resulting in the right way of living, it misses the point. The people believed their gathered meeting of songs, prayers, and sacrifices put them in good standing with God. The shortcoming of this pillar of their faith was critical. Israel gathered as God's people, but failed to live as God's people.

Sabbath

The second pillar of Judaism Jesus challenged was the Sabbath. His healing on the Sabbath day caused an intense reaction. For us, it is hard to relate to healing someone on the Sabbath as being such a huge deal. Rooted in the Ten Commandments, the Sabbath was a major distinctive of what it meant to be Jewish. In the cultures around Israel, it was a radical idea to take a day off. God's command that the Sabbath be extended to servants and animals was even more unprecedented. The directive to keep the day holy by not working presented many questions. As a result, man-made laws numbering in the hundreds were established, defining what violates the no-work rule. How far one could walk (a Sabbath day's journey), and not kindling a fire, sewing, or writing were but a few of their forbidden activities for the Sabbath. The following Scripture passage reveals the reaction to Jesus for healing on the Sabbath:

> Again he entered the synagogue, and a man was there with a withered hand. And they watched Jesus, to see whether he would heal him on the Sabbath, so that they might accuse him. And he said to the man with the withered hand, "Come here." And he said to them, "Is it lawful on the Sabbath to do good or to do harm, to save life or to kill?" But they were silent. And he looked around at them with anger, grieved at their hardness of heart, and said to the man, "Stretch out your hand." He stretched it out, and his hand was restored. The Pharisees went out and immediately held counsel with the Herodians against him, how to destroy him. (Mark 3:1–6)

Response to Jesus

Although it was permissible to suspend the no-work rule of the Sabbath to save life, making someone well was prohibited. To save life was one thing, but to make someone better could wait until the Sabbath was over. The point of the Sabbath was not how carefully one avoided working. Jesus taught that the Sabbath was made for man, not man for the Sabbath. It was a gift; God derives no benefit from our not working. He wants us to rest, get out from under the pressure, and take time for the re-creation of the soul. He wants us to focus on higher pursuits than acquiring the stuff of this world. To do so makes the Sabbath a day dedicated unto the Lord.

The Old Testament prophet Amos challenged Israel's observance of the Sabbath as failing to influence who they were and how they lived:

> Hear this, you who trample on the needy and bring the poor of the land to an end, saying, 'When will the new moon be over, that we may sell grain? And the Sabbath, that we may offer wheat for sale, that we may make the ephah small and the shekel great and deal deceitfully with false balances, that we may buy the poor for silver and the needy for a pair of sandals and sell the chaff of the wheat?' (Amos 8:4–6)

Israel kept the Sabbath, yet lived in ways dishonorable to God. Sadly, Christianity has the same reputation. It is a common critique given by outsiders that followers of Jesus are a discredit to the faith they profess.

It is no small thing that Mark 3 describes Jesus looking at the crowd with anger, grieved at their hardness of heart as they waited to see if he would heal the man with the withered hand. Compassion for the one needing to be healed was nowhere to be found. Thinking that God's nature is such that healing on the Sabbath offends him and that anyone doing so deserves to die was the worst portrait of God anyone could paint. Their confidence, thinking they knew God when they didn't, brought him grief.

In like fashion, making a whip and forcefully disrupting the moneymaking transactions at the temple was an equal display of concern. Stripping the poor of what little resources they had and portraying the rituals at the temple as what mattered the most to God was an abomination in the eyes of Jesus.

Failure to know God and live in his presence, guided by his authority and empowered by his Spirit, is the worst of mistakes. Thinking that God is satisfied when we participate in religious events is to replace the God of love with an inferior and mistaken concept.

A New Approach

After the death, resurrection, and ascension of Jesus, the early church faced many questions concerning how to move forward. The temple sacrifices had been brought to completion. Also, in honor of his resurrection, the early church made the first day of the week rather than the Sabbath as the day for their meetings. At first, the need to meet with one another was a means of surviving persecution. Throughout the week, eating a meal around the Lord's table was a lifeline. The need to support one another emotionally, spiritually, and financially drew God's people together in bonds of love. Church for them was truly a source of life.

The expansion of Christianity into Gentile regions brought new churches into being. The apostle Paul was the dominant voice of instruction for the spiritual development of these groups. Over time, under the inspiration of the Holy Spirit, guidelines were established for how the church was to function. Paul's letter to the church at Corinth addresses God's intention for his people as a gathered assembly.

The situation at Corinth was not good. What was going on in this church was a discredit to the faith. Corinth was a seaport town having the reputation of recklessly pursuing pleasure. Various temples to the gods were available, with the predominant one being to Aphrodite, offering one thousand female prostitutes. Divisiveness, incest, immorality, denial of the resurrection, and failure to live the way of love as taught and exampled by Jesus were present within this church.

Manifestations of the Spirit were an issue dividing the church. Pride and unkindness surrounded the visible signs of the working of God. In addressing this issue, Paul instructed the church to preeminently pursue the way of love:

> If I speak in the tongues of men and of angels, but have not love, I am a noisy gong or a clanging cymbal. And if I have prophetic powers, and understand all mysteries and all knowledge, and if I have all faith, so as to remove mountains, but have not love, I am nothing. If I give away all

I have, and if I deliver up my body to be burned, but have not love, I gain nothing. (1 Cor. 13:1–3)

Some in the church at Corinth were taking pride in certain expressions of the Spirit, while at the same time counting those without these gifts as inferior in the faith. Paul's response to this violation of the way of love gives insight into God's design for how his people are to live together.

In 1 Corinthians 12, Paul speaks to the church about spiritual gifting within the body of believers. First, God does not gift each person the same. There are a variety of gifts, ways to serve, and activities of the Spirit. Second, each person is given a manifestation of the Spirit for the common good. Third, all of this is as God wills—not earned nor achieved.

This design for how Spirit life works parallels life in the physical. We are all wired differently. Some are farmers, healthcare workers, engineers, and educators, while others are artists, carpenters, and public servants. Our individuality makes for the community being able to benefit from our differences. Spirit life works in a similar way.

Paul's response to the issue of spiritual gifting is quite instructive. In comparing the members of the church to the different parts of our body, Paul identifies an error being expressed in two opposite poles. Those with visible gifting considered themselves to be special, even to the point of saying: "I do not need you." On the other hand, those without these gifts felt, "I do not belong. I'm not needed." Paul rebuked the first group by asking, "What do you have that you did not receive as a gift?" To the second group, Paul instructed them to not minimize God's choice of giving them a manifestation of the Spirit that is less visible. Each person is gifted for the common good of the body; therefore, to say you are of no value is to discount the role God has chosen for you. One can have stewardship over a gift that is not visible, but it does not mean that it is not life-giving. The parts of our physical body that are not visible are those which sustain life for us.

God has put the church together as a community benefiting from our differences that are essential to the whole. When we live as individuals attending a church event, God's goal is not achieved.

This concept of how the church should function is rooted in the prayer of Jesus at the Last Supper: "I in them and you in me, that they may become perfectly one, so that the world may know that you sent me and loved them even as you loved me" (John 17:23). Being in the same building with a group of people that you do not know and have no desire to be connected with is not the relational unity Jesus prayed for.

As a follower of Jesus, taking the initiative to be interconnected with your church body as a means of growing spiritually and bringing glory to God is the way of love. Anything less is to miss the point of God's intention for his people to gather.

Joining Together as Family

A second dimension of how Spirit life works is that we become God's children by being born again. The apostle John wrote, "In this the love of God was made manifest among us, that God sent his only Son into the world, so that we might live through him" (1 John 4:9). "See what kind of love the Father has given to us, that we should be called the children of God; and so we are. . . . Beloved, we are God's children now, and what we will be has not yet appeared; but we know that when he appears we shall be like him because we shall see him as he is. And everyone who thus hopes in him purifies himself as he is pure" (1 John 3:1–3).

Taking a moment to follow John's line of thinking is important. Presenting the Creator of the universe as willing to become involved in our lives is mind-blowing. Further, that he loves us to the point of giving his Son that we might live is even more unexpected. Reaching even higher, if we respond to him, we become his children.

The apostle Paul also speaks of God's great desire for us to be his children. "But when the fullness of time had come, God sent forth his Son, born of woman, born under the law, to redeem those who were under the law, so that we might receive adoption as sons. . . . So you are no longer a slave, but a son, and if a son, then an heir through God" (Gal. 4:4–5, 7). Sadly, his word picture of someone being sold as a slave was a scene very familiar to his audience. Without question, redeeming a slave in order to adopt him as a son was outside any normal expectation.

Imagine the thoughts of a slave as he hears the gavel fall and the announcement: "Sold!" Once again, he has no hope, no future, no rights. The uncertainty of what his new master will be like and the nature of his living arrangement looms over him. As they walk away from the auction, the slave asks, "Where will I live? What will I be doing?"

The answer is given: "You will live with me. I have redeemed you so that I could adopt you. You will inherit all I have. You are no longer a slave. You are my son!" Any attempt to capture the slave's response to what he has heard is out of reach. The gift given to him is beyond anything imaginable. This is what God has done for us. He paid the price for our redemption in order to bring us into his family. If the magnitude of God's gift of love doesn't totally blow your mind, you are not paying attention.

God established his church not as an event to attend, but rather as a place for his family to gather. Culturally, we have an endless array of things that cast us into a spectator role. Movies, entertainment, and sporting events separate people into professional participants and paying spectators. Church is not a spectator event. God intends for his church to be a living entity of relationships enriching each other's lives.

The wealth of wisdom and experience in living out the faith available in a body of believers is accessible only when we live together as a family. The failure to be a family of believers, interconnected and growing together, is an issue in churches regardless of the size.

Family is not easy. As kids mature heartbreaking issues emerge; and as older family members age, it is a test of love to meet their needs. Being a family means looking to the interests of others rather than ourselves. Family works only when love is present. Learning to love is God's goal for us.

Church is the place where you go if you need to cry or want to rejoice. It is the place to feel safe and get the strength needed to deal with life. It is the source of inspiration to live life well. When a crisis hits, needs arise, and it feels as if the world is falling apart, it is our church family who shares our perspective on life and, therefore, can be the most help.

There is a huge difference in going to church and being a family. Church is something you are, as opposed to something you attend. It requires knowing folks and their struggles and being there with them through the challenges of life.

In many churches, small groups are offered as a means of family life. Whether the design of small groups goes far enough to accomplish family life is an important question. Usually, small groups are formed around folks in the same station of life—moms with small children, college students meeting together, etc.

When grandmas are put in a separate room and talk about the faucet that leaks or the door that won't shut, who is among them to say, "When can I come and fix it for you?" Also, a wealth of wisdom and opportunity to love is lost when grandmas and young moms don't have the opportunity to spend time together building relationships of mutual love and appreciation.

When I was a twenty-year-old preparing to go into a combat zone, it was the older, battle-hardened veterans that we spent time with. The military did not leave us in a room by ourselves to try to figure out what we should do when our plane landed in Southeast Asia. Similarly, college kids need exposure to those who are fighting the good fight of the faith. They need to hear from those who have endured the attacks of Satan on their marriage, faith, and purity before the Lord. They need to sit with folks who have wisdom that has been refined in the furnace of life. The model for maturity in life and in faith requires exposure to the whole family. Certainly, young folks need to meet together, but to do so is not adequate preparation to enter a combat zone. Family life is not achieved by separation, and the occasion to love and be loved is lost when the whole family does not come to the table. Otherwise, are we not saying: "I do not want to be bothered or need to be around the entire family?"

Jesus put his life on the line challenging the idea that simply attending temple or keeping the Sabbath was a means of having a relationship with our heavenly Father. At the end of the day, we can simply be involved in a religious event, or we can find the mutually life-changing dimension of walking through life with our brothers and sisters in Christ.

As Paul closed out his letter to the Romans, he mentions more than thirty people by name. The comments he makes about each of them are heartwarming and are a vivid example of how the body of Christ is supposed to function. He speaks of those who are helpers, others who have risked their lives for him, fellow prisoners, and how the mother of Rufus is also a mother to him. He not only knows these people, but he has a relationship with each of them that he values and depends upon.

The question before church leadership is whether it is important or even necessary to follow the biblical model for the gathered meeting of God's people. Based on the teaching of Scripture, it seems appropriate to ask whether our present structure for church promotes God's people being drawn into mutually benefiting relationships across the entire spectrum of his family.

Jesus rejected the misplaced emphasis of the temple and the man-made structure for observing the Sabbath. He presented the goal for the gathered community of believers in the following scene described in Mark's gospel:

> And his mother and brothers came, and standing outside they sent to him and called him. And a crowd was sitting around him, and they said to him, "Your mother and your brothers are outside, seeking you." And he answered them, "Who are my mother and my brothers?" And looking about at those who sat around him, he said, "Here are my mother

and my brothers! For whoever does the will of God, he is my brother and sister and mother." (Mark 3:31–35)

For many, the decision to follow Jesus caused a division between them and their family. Even here in this scene of Jesus being sought by his mother and siblings, their motivation was based on an inappropriate concern for him. "And when his family heard it, they went out to seize him, for they were saying, 'He is out of his mind'" (Mark 3:21). Jesus pointed those around him to the bonds of family on a higher plane found among those who seek God's will for their lives.

Does modern church life promote the development of this level of relationships among its people? Are our buildings full of strangers in a crowd with giftings not utilized for the common good and with needs not met? Being satisfied with attending a church event rather than giving the time and commitment to be family is to miss God's intention for his people. Each of us have been gifted spiritually for the common good of the body. Failure to be responsible with our personal gifting is to live short of what God intends for us and how we can serve others.

For Jesus, attending temple and observing the Sabbath brought people together without achieving God's goal for them. We are faced with the challenge to not make the same mistake.

A Word of Encouragement

Gathering as God's people while failing to live as God's people is the worst of mistakes. God intends for his people to be a living entity of relationships enriching and encouraging each other's lives. Being loved, cared for, and having a safe place to work through life's challenges is what God intends for his gathered community of believers.

CHAPTER 5

TEACHER

The effectiveness of Jesus as a teacher is limited by our willingness to be students. For some, his teaching was confusing; for others, he taught with an authority touching the soul.
—Ed Malone

ANSWERING THE CALL TO FOLLOW JESUS IS LIFE-CHANGing. It is the experience of the fullness of life, and it fulfills the purpose of our existence. Following Jesus goes beyond believing something about his life. It is more than attending church events. It is to live in a spiritual relationship with him, extending his mission of doing the will of the Father as a servant of the kingdom. If we know him and abide in him, we will follow his commands and live as he lived. In previous chapters, we have explored how he lived and what he was passionate about. We now turn to him as our teacher.

Referring to someone as a good teacher usually means they are entertaining, hold your attention, offer insightful thoughts, have a unique delivery style, or leave you with a lot to think about. Jesus presented his message in a variety of ways. He crafted parables set in everyday life to demonstrate spiritual truths. His ability to quiet his opponents with a simple question demonstrated wisdom beyond comparison. Often, he left the listener to decide whether he was speaking literally or spiritually. In personal encounters, his teaching was sometimes specific to the individual, while at other times he presented universal truths. In some situations, his words made one's head spin.

Jesus caused quite a stir when he said that we must eat his flesh and drink his blood and hate our mother and father to follow him. His call to turn the cheek, go the second mile, and refuse not him who begs came across equally confusing. Telling those around him that if your hand offends you, cut it off, and that he came not to bring peace but a sword was more than many could receive.

For followers of Jesus, the Gospels give the opportunity to hear him teach. The occasions when it was difficult to understand him were intentional. Having to work through what he taught, utilizing the Spirit's help, is a good thing. His difficult sayings were far from the norm. For the bulk of his teaching, Jesus spoke painfully clear. Not understanding him is not the issue, but being willing to follow what he said. If we are not diligent students, it doesn't matter how well he taught or the power of his words. Jesus referring to those around him as disciples was quite instructive.

Among the Jewish people, the concept of discipleship was common. John the Baptist, the Pharisees, and the rabbis had disciples. A disciple was a learner, a student, one committed to embracing the priorities and teachings of the one they chose to follow.

Being a disciple in first-century Israel meant leaving one's family to travel from place to place in often sparse conditions. The commitment of a disciple was to absorb the teaching of his rabbi so that his wisdom would live on through them as his disciple. One could not choose to be a disciple, but rather went through an application process before being accepted into the circle of disciples. Discipleship was for the elite few—for seasoned adherents of the faith and for those willing to invest their whole life in following a particular teacher. A rabbi taught through questions, pressing the disciple to investigate the meaning of words, traditions, and real-life issues of the faith. The disciple was not given answers to memorize, but was challenged to learn how to understand the why behind the principles of faith and life.

Before ascending back to the Father, Jesus said, "Go therefore and make disciples of all nations, baptizing them in the name of the Father and of the Son and of the Holy Spirit, teaching them to observe all that I have commanded you. And behold, I am with you always, to the end of the age" (Matt. 28:19–20).

There were similarities and yet challenging distinctions between the Jewish form of discipleship and what Jesus offered. In the Jewish form, only the elite could pass the application process. Not everyone could be a disciple. It created a superiority between disciples and ordinary believers. On the other hand, Jesus invites everyone to be his disciple. He will train and develop his disciples rather than their having to gain approval first. With Jesus, everyone accepting the call to follow him is a disciple. In a similar teaching style of a rabbi, Jesus taught by parables and asked a lot of questions, encouraging the listener to search for understanding. With Jesus, discipleship was more than being a believer, a convert, a church member, or one who attends meetings. His disciples were to absorb his teaching as a means of living out his message in pursuit of the fullness of life and as a witness to the world. As stated earlier, professing Christians who can't name five parables that Jesus taught or events out of his life that they treasure and use to model how they live stands quite distant from any consideration of being his disciples. Discipleship is not an optional second tier of being a Christian. Jesus did not say to go into the world and make Christians who have the option to go to the next level of being disciples.

Discipleship is a lifelong process of conformity to Jesus. A disciple is guided by the Word of God and empowered spiritually, living among a community of believers committed to living out their faith. A disciple is one who wrestles with the Scriptures to apply them to life. Jesus pointed people to the Word, asking not only what it said, but also asking how they understood it. It was common for Jesus to answer a question with a question.

Jesus called those around him to discipleship, and he left the commission for his followers to go into the world and make disciples, and yet the call to be a disciple of Jesus is only mentioned in the Gospels and the book of Acts. Later, New Testament writers, approaching a Gentile world unfamiliar with the Jewish concept of discipleship, used different descriptors for being a follower of Jesus.

In Acts 11 we are told that the disciples were first called Christians at Antioch. When Paul was on trial, King Agrippa said, "In a short time would you persuade me to be a Christian?" (Acts 26:28). When Paul wrote his letters to the churches, he addressed the Christians as saints. For example, Paul, in his letter to the church at Corinth wrote, "To the church of God that is in Corinth, to those sanctified in Christ Jesus, called to be saints together with all those who in every place call upon the name of our Lord Jesus Christ" (1 Cor. 1:2).

Calling followers of Jesus disciples, Christians, saints, brothers and sisters, the body of Christ, the temple of the Holy Spirit, and family are companion terms coming together to enlarge our understanding of the commitment we have made to Jesus. These descriptors are not optional levels of commitment, but rather are attempts to identify the full ramification of our new life in Christ. Together they form a collage of concepts worthy of our identification with Jesus.

The reference to followers of Jesus being Christians is, perhaps, the most difficult to live up to. Being Christlike should certainly be our goal and responsibility because, after all, we must bear witness to him. The designation of being saints is the dominant reference made in the New Testament for the people of God. Over the history of Catholicism, "saint" became the identifier for people of exceptional holiness or those accomplishing great things for the kingdom. Today many proclaim, "I'm no saint!" However, Paul writes, "To all those in Rome who are loved by God and called to be saints" (Rom. 1:7).

Saints are called to holiness—being set apart from the evil ways of the world in dedication to God's service. Just as God is love, he is holy. We are to reflect his glory to our world. Peter describes this part of our calling quite well: "His divine power has granted to us all things that pertain to life and godliness, through the knowledge of him who called us to his own glory and excellence, by which he has granted to us his precious and very great promises, so that through them you may become partakers of the divine nature, having escaped from the corruption that is in the world because of sinful desire" (2 Pet. 1:3–4).

Whether as a disciple (a student of his Master) or a saint (set apart to share in God's holiness), we must learn from Jesus as our teacher. His teaching is the means of our being transformed into his likeness, breaking away from conformity to our world. It is the way we learn how to live in God's kingdom.

Hard, Complex, and Layered Sayings

When Jesus said, "If your right hand causes you to sin, cut it off. . . . For it is better that you lose one of your members than that your whole body go into hell" (Matt. 5:30), these words caused uneasiness for all who listened to him. First, your hand does not cause you to sin. Cutting off your hand does not fix the problem. Jesus said in Mark 7:20–23, "What comes out of a person is what defiles him. For from within, out of the heart of man, come evil thoughts, sexual immorality, theft, murder, adultery, coveting, wickedness, deceit, sensuality, envy, slander, pride, foolishness. All these things come from within, and they defile a person." The problem of sin resides not in the hand, but in the heart. His use of hyperbole (exaggeration) was to draw attention to not letting anything, even if it is your right hand, stand in your way of entering the kingdom or dealing with sin.

Equal to the statement of cutting off your hand if it offends you is, "If anyone comes to me and does not hate his own father and mother . . .he cannot be my disciple" (Luke 14:26). The English translation doesn't do justice to what Jesus was saying. Hating is a Semitic expression that means to love less. Matthew 10:37 presents the intent of this teaching more clearly. Loving your parents more than Jesus was his point. For some, being rejected by their family was at stake in following Jesus. That is why Jesus said, "Do you think I have come to give peace on earth? No, I tell you, but rather division" (Luke 12:51). Many homes were divided over the acceptance of Jesus. The issue stressed here is a lordship commitment to Jesus, which rises above anyone or anything.

When Jesus told the rich young ruler in Mark 10:21 to sell all that he had, give to the poor, and follow him, it was not a universal calling for all followers of Jesus. This was a specific command to this individual because money held an unholy place in his life—it was his god. If this were a blanket requirement of the kingdom, God's people would be penniless and dependent on the grace of others to live. Instead, Jesus gave specific instructions in Matthew 6 concerning giving alms to the needy. Also, Jesus taught in Matthew 25 that his followers are to clothe the naked, feed the hungry, and take the homeless poor into their houses. The ability to meet the needs of others requires having possessions and exercising stewardship over one's money rather than giving it away all at once. The issue of ownership of our lives and all we have certainly belongs to our Lord. Our lives and our possessions are to be made available for his use.

In Matthew 8:19, a scribe expressed a willingness to follow Jesus, saying, "Teacher, I will follow you wherever you go." Keying in on the scribe's use of the word *wherever*, Jesus responded in verse 20, "Foxes have holes, and birds of the air have nests, but the Son of Man has nowhere to lay his head." Jesus was forthright in telling the scribe that following him wherever can be costly.

In verse 21, a second individual requested, "Lord, let me first go and bury my father." Jesus said to him, "Follow me, and leave the dead to bury their own dead" (v. 22). Since the dead cannot bury the dead, we are certainly pointed to a spiritual application of his response. The man's statement ("Lord, let me first") makes following Jesus secondary to other things. Jesus framed his response as to the priority required in following him in a way that caught everyone's attention. Jesus unquestionably expected his followers to honor their parents.

In a different setting, Jesus said, "You have a fine way of rejecting the commandment of God in order to establish your tradition! For Moses said, 'Honor your father and your mother'; and, 'Whoever reviles father or mother must surely die.' But you say, 'If a man tells his father or his mother, "Whatever you would have gained from me is Corban"' (that is, given to God)—then you no longer permit him to do anything for his father or mother, thus making void the word of

God by your tradition that you have handed down. And many such things you do" (Mark 7:9–13).

The point Jesus made with these two would-be followers and the rich ruler is that following him supersedes anything or anyone and can be costly. These hard sayings require some investigation and familiarization with his total message in order to discern the truth Jesus was presenting. The listener must be a diligent student in order not to draw the wrong conclusion.

Deny, Take Up, Follow

The call Jesus gave in Mark 8 provoked some additional hard questions. "And calling the crowd to him with his disciples, he said to them, 'If anyone would come after me, let him deny himself and take up his cross and follow me. For whoever would save his life will lose it, but whoever loses his life for my sake and the gospel's will save it'" (Mark 8:34–35). When one groups the calling to deny self, take up our cross, and follow Jesus with him saying that he came to give life and give it in abundance—it creates questions. One part of his teaching sounds hard and costly, while the other describes a huge blessing. How are both true at the same time?

The paradox of losing life by saving it means that we can hold on to our selfish lives and in turn miss out on eternal life. The denial of our selfish nature is a good thing—to do so brings life. It indeed brings a challenge, but one worth meeting. Our selfishness is an opening for the devil to lure us into traps, bringing death.

Taking up our cross daily means to live out the Father's will. Jesus faced the cross with these words, "Not as I will, but as you will" (Matt. 26:39). Taking up our cross indicates that there is an option that we must choose in yielding to the will of the Father, which will be expressed in each of our lives in unique ways. Spending time with him enables us to get in touch with his plan for us. Taking up our cross daily is a call to be continually in touch with the Father's specific will for our lives. Through denial of our selfish desires and willingness to do his will, we are in a position to follow him.

Following Jesus as a servant is the broad category out of which we accomplish his will for our lives. In Mark 9, the disciples argued with one another about who was the greatest. Jesus said, "If anyone would be first, he must be last of all and servant of all" (Mark 9:35). In response to James and John asking to sit one on his left hand and the other on his right hand as places of privilege and authority, Jesus said, "You know that those who are considered rulers of the Gentiles lord it over them, and their great ones exercise authority over them. But it shall not be so among you. But whoever would be great among you must be your servant, and whoever would be first among you must be slave of all. For even the Son of Man came not to be served but to serve, and to give his life as a ransom for many" (Mark 10:42–45). As demonstrated by Jesus, the call to be a servant knows no boundaries. He certainly set no limits as a servant to the will of the Father. In equality with God, he laid down his privileges to live as a man, serving the will of the Father in securing our salvation by his death. Finding life by being a servant depends on embracing the words of Jesus, that "It is more blessed to give than to receive" (Acts 20:35).

How Do You Read?

When a lawyer asked Jesus what he must do to inherit eternal life, Jesus said, "What is written in the law? How do you read it?" (Luke 10:26). The lawyer responded by quoting the great commandment— love God and your neighbor as yourself. The lawyer had the right answer, but not the right understanding. In response to the lawyer's question, "And who is my neighbor?", Jesus told the story of the good Samaritan.

As the story goes, a man traveling from Jerusalem to Jericho fell among thieves and was robbed and beaten. A priest passed by the man on the other side of the road. A Levite (a lay associate of the priest) passed by the man as well. A Samaritan (people hated by the Jews) stopped to help him. He poured oil and wine on his wounds, put him on his beast while he walked to an inn, and cared for him. Upon leaving, he gave the innkeeper money to continue his care and committed to paying the innkeeper if there were additional expenses. The obvious point of the story is that my neighbor is anyone needing my help. The Jewish people felt obligated to help a fellow Jew but not anyone else. The details Jesus gave in telling this story present a deeper challenge. The Samaritan was not just helpful, but went well beyond any reasonable expectation in caring for the man beaten by the robbers.

The question of who my neighbor is allowed Jesus to address more than the man was asking. Jesus challenged the Jewish lack of caring for anyone but a fellow Jew, and then he defined what true kindness looks like from God's perspective. Jesus gave a simple story that carried a profound message.

The Sower

The parable of the sower is another example of how we can be shortsighted in comprehending the teaching of Jesus. As recorded in Mark 4 and Matthew 13, Jesus gave the story of a farmer sowing seed. The seed was good, and therefore, the intended harvest was dependent upon the quality of the soil. Four different soil types are described.

When Jesus was alone with his disciples, he asked if they understood his parable. He explained that Satan's interference, a shallow response to the Word, the cares of the world, and desires for other things prevent the seed from being fruitful. Many use this parable to describe why people do not respond to the Word of the kingdom. However, if the parable is only about getting saved, why is there a repeated emphasis on a hundredfold harvest?

Picturing a farmer scattering seed was easy. Recognizing that the soil affects the harvest was a principle of agriculture known by all who were listening. However, when Jesus announced the potential of a hundredfold harvest, every farmer in the crowd would have been eager to hear more. All listening would have gladly rejoiced with even a tenfold harvest. Jesus explained the good soil as being those who hear, accept the Word into their lives, and in turn bear fruit. This three-step response of hearing, accepting, and bearing fruit is God's goal for our lives.

Just as the devil works to prevent people from hearing and accepting the Word, he also strives to keep the Word from bearing fruit. A shallow response to the Word is not enough to enter the kingdom, and it also prevents fruit production. Distracting desires and cares of the world choke out our proper response to the kingdom, as well as hinder fruit-bearing.

Thinking of myself as good soil because I have heard and accepted the Word of the kingdom is not the full intention of this parable. Soil can be good at one point, even yielding fruit, but soil can become unproductive. The same barriers of a shallow life and/or a life full of competing desires eliminate fruit-bearing. All the teaching Jesus gave about Spirit life either thrives or dies according to the nature of the soil of our hearts and lives.

Our Way of Life

How would an outside observer describe the American way of life? Fast-paced and stress-filled with not enough time to get everything done would probably top the list. An obsession with shopping and eating out would probably take an easy second. The American way of life typically involves fragmented families with everyone going in different directions such that family meals, including time for conversation, are a rare event. Life is so fast-paced that a time-management secretary is needed for each household to keep track of all that is going on. Constantly seeking fun and excitement afforded by our extravagant lifestyle captures what many in our culture describe as living the good life. Electronic relationships, instant gratification, and the constant need to be entertained certainly need to be included as identifiers of the nature of life in our world. According to Jesus, the Word of the kingdom cannot flourish in such an environment. He would describe us as being those who live on the path with weeds so high that we cannot see the proper way to go as we chase after competing desires.

Farmers apply lime to balance the pH of the soil and add fertilizer to increase the level of nutrients needed. Spiritually, we must do the same. Limestone rock being ground up to make lime and being applied to the soil can be compared to our need to have a constant application of the rock of Jesus in our lives. Emphasis on me makes my life acidic. Emphasis on God brings me back into balance. Dead, organic materials can be turned into fertilizer. Leaves and food scraps that have passed through a mulching process are an excellent way to feed the garden. Followers of Jesus understand that the death of self is material God uses to fertilize the soil of our lives.

Parables are more than stories. They are vehicles of spiritual truth. Those willing to spiritually explore the truth in the parable benefit greatly.

The central teaching conveyed by this parable is that the fruitfulness of the seed is dependent on the condition of the soil. The choices we make about our pace of living, competing desires, and shallow commitment prevent the fruitful outcome of the seed of God's Word. Many read something in the Scriptures or hear inspiring teaching with a commitment to follow through with that concept in their lives. However, it doesn't take long for the devil to take the thought from us as it lands on the hardened path of our lives or dies due to the lack of nourishment because of the shallowness of our lives before God. Additionally, life's competing desires choke out our good intentions. Not only is this a parable about why folks do not receive the Word of God unto salvation, but why we fail to have fruit through our lives to the glory of God. Parables such as this one can bring life to the student who is diligently seeking the truth.

Utilizing the backdrop of a disciple with his master as a model for following Jesus, a disciple is first and foremost a student. Anyone who claims to follow Jesus without being his student is fumbling around in the dark. In the designation of followers of Jesus being saints, we are set apart unto the holiness of God. If this is true, our lives reflect God's kingdom rather than the world.

In first-century Judaism, selection as a disciple was huge. One would spend years preparing before seeking an appointment of discipleship. The living conditions were extremely sparse. Answering the rabbi's questions and studying constantly were one's way of life. So what was the driving force?

At some point, the potential disciple had been exposed to the wisdom, insight, and knowledge base of a particular rabbi. His teaching had stirred a longing within the listener's heart to go deeper into the mystery of the faith. No amount of hard work or sacrifice was too much to ask for the opportunity to be with the rabbi he admired.

Alongside this concept, Jesus, the Son of God, possessing all wisdom and knowledge, extends the opportunity of discipleship to all who have a willing heart. It doesn't matter if you are not the smartest in the group, but only that your heart longs to know the deep things of God. For some people, it is truly the opportunity of a lifetime to be constantly under his teaching and guidance.

Many professing Christians consider listening to a twenty-minute talk once a week more than enough time spent on spiritual matters. If they have a few minutes of free time, the last thing they would consider doing would be to study and meditate on the things of God. Having Jesus available 24/7 is not something that drives their lives. C. S. Lewis says that humanity is far too easily entertained. Sadly, he seems to be very accurate in his assessment.

Classrooms are full of students listening to the same teacher with different results. An eager student will one day teach the class or use the knowledge for great results. Many do not have ears with which to hear and therefore, cannot wait for class to be over. How often and with what level of desire do you sit at the feet of Jesus listening to him teach as you depend upon him to guide you home?

A Word of Encouragement

With the Spirit's help, there is more available in the teaching Jesus gave than surface appearances. A diligent student seeks to be a credit to his master.

CHAPTER 6

WEEDS DON'T NEED ANY HELP

In the parable of the sower, addressed in the previous chapter, Jesus spoke of weeds competing with a farmer's effort of sowing seed. His metaphor addresses an important spiritual principle of the kingdom of God.
—Ed Malone

WITH THE INDUSTRIALIZATION OF AMERICA, OUR modern generation has lost contact with the land. Therefore, Jesus using weeds as an illustration has lost some of its power—but it's extremely effective when properly understood. I offer the following as a means of demonstrating the point Jesus was making.

Unexpected Shock

A few years ago, I had the opportunity to rent a farm nearby. A couple of the back fields had been lying fallow for a while. As a result of this neglect, the fields were a mess. For three years, I managed those fields by mowing appropriately and adding nutrients to the soil through the application of fertilizer. The fruit of my labor was a nice stand of grass yielding a much-valued hay crop. As my daddy often said, "The grass in this field is as thick as the hair on a dog's back."

The owner then decided to rent to another farmer, so for several years someone else had control of those fields. At one point, the new renter contacted me about harvesting hay on a portion of the

73

land. As a gesture of appreciation, I volunteered to do some mowing around the farm.

Harvesting hay requires many trips through a field, bringing familiarity with every little bump, hole, and change of elevation. The back fields ran along a spring-fed creek, and during the fall the fence-rows were lined with trees changing colors. I was eager to see the land that I had worked for several years.

As I made my way through the woods and across the big drainage ditch and rode up in full view of the back field, I was overwhelmed. Weeds and thorns had covered it—with no grass in sight! I didn't expect to see the land struggling under the weight of this invasion of weeds. It hadn't been that long ago when the field was healthy and strong.

Like a military tank armed for battle, my tractor pushed relentlessly through the field. Weeds stood high enough to block my view, and hordes of insects pounded me in the face as I mowed. After a couple of laps around the field, pollen and grass seed covered both the tractor and me in a yellow blanket. Eventually, as the land began to clear, I could see a stand of grass that was fighting to stay alive. At the end of the day, the field was clean.

As I sat on my tractor looking across the newly mown field, I knew the battle had only begun. It would take fertilizer and the addition of clover grasses to give the extra punch needed for the grass to fully recover. Weed seeds had been scattered, and more weeds would come back from their root system. Some people, considering the magnitude of the problem, would have filled a sprayer and given the weeds what they deserved. However, since I am a Vietnam veteran dealing with aftereffects of Agent Orange, I try to manage my fields in ways other than blasting them with chemicals.

Uninvited Destruction

Weeds flourish without any assistance and do not need an invitation to show up in a field. All they need is for someone to neglect the grass. Weeds also grow at the speed of light. That is why old folks used

74

to say the kids were "growing like weeds." In a matter of days, weeds can rise above the grass and shade out the sunlight. Unmanaged weeds take the lion's share of any available nutrients and moisture. Soon, the grass has no chance.

Jesus explained the competing power of weeds when he said, "And others are the ones sown among thorns. They are those who hear the Word, but the cares of the world and the deceitfulness of riches and the desires for other things enter in and choke the word, and it proves unfruitful" (Mark 4:18–19). The call of the kingdom needs to be protected, or the weeds will choke out the stirring of God within us. If we allow weeds to take over, the only thing in life that matters—our opportunity to be in God's kingdom—will be destroyed.

Taking Action

The battle with weeds in the kingdom of God is a familiar one for seasoned Christians. Like the field I mowed, there is the constant need to clean up our lives by confession and repentance. Confession is to agree with God that an action was wrong. Repentance is to be sorry for what was done and to commit to change. God's forgiveness cleanses the field of the weeds.

Clearing the field is the proper first step, but seeds and root systems are in place that will bring new weeds. There is a lot to do before the battle with weeds is brought under control.

With the purchase of our farm, we inherited a crop of thistles, ironweed, buttercup, and cockleburs scattered throughout the fields. Every time a cocklebur picked up its head, I would cut it off. Mowing cockleburs before they turn to seed is an effective control measure because it breaks their seed cycle. However, since thistles come back from their root systems, my wife, Gale, continually walks our farm with a shovel in her hand on a crusade to take out by the roots every thistle with the audacity to spread its seed. Buttercups are about to make me break my no-chemical ban because I'm not sure I'll ever be free of them otherwise.

In terms of the kingdom, repentance, confession, and forgiveness are the places to start, but the weeds are going to come back. We must stay alert to cut off any competing desire before it has a chance to grow. Some issues are deeply rooted and require a shovel if they're to be eliminated.

For example, Jesus said that the battle with adultery must be cut off with the first appearance of lust. Even deeper than lust is the question of whether we think that we are being deprived of something good outside of the commands of God. In Genesis 3, the serpent convinced Eve that God was keeping something good from her that eating the forbidden fruit would provide. Questioning God's character in this way is a common mistake still with us today.

Competing desires seek to unseat God's preeminence in our lives. The weeds of worry and the deceitfulness of wealth challenge our trust in God. The mistaken desire to find life in ways other than in the kingdom questions God's desire to give us life.

Some weeds are controlled by breaking the seed cycle, while others have to come out by the roots. Still other weeds flourish because of a failure to take care of the soil.

Sour Ground

In our part of the country, sage grass turns a golden brown in the fall. It stands up tall and looks pretty, but cows don't eat it. When old farmers see a stand of sage grass, they say, "You've got some sour ground there." The technical explanation is that the pH is out of balance. When the soil is too acidic, sage grass takes over. The solution is to make the soil more alkaline with the application of lime (calcium carbonate). When the soil is balanced properly, good grasses can grow.

John the Baptist told his disciples that he had to decrease while Jesus increased. The concept of Jesus being in us works a lot like balancing the pH of the soil. When the "I" in my life is out of balance with the control Jesus should have, then the soil of my life gets sour, and weeds have a great opportunity to thrive. However, when Jesus is allowed to increase, the pH is balanced properly, and the good grasses of the kingdom can grow.

Early Detection

Weeds stand out clearly when one is interested in producing grass. When I walk my fields, I am keenly aware of the level of clover grasses that produce nitrogen to promote grass production. Also, I constantly monitor the level of good grasses that will produce the rich protein my cows need. Weeds are like neon signs to a conscientious farmer.

Paul said, "We destroy arguments and every lofty opinion raised against the knowledge of God, and take every thought captive to obey Christ" (2 Cor. 10:5). The discipline of addressing our thoughts to make them obedient to Christ can have revolutionary results if you approach the kingdom this way; weeds will be removed before they can gain a death grip on your spiritual walk.

In Galatians 5, Paul provides a list identifying the fruit of the Spirit as opposed to the fruit of the selfish nature: "Now the works of the flesh are evident: sexual immorality, impurity, sensuality, idolatry, sorcery, enmity, strife, jealousy, fits of anger, rivalries, dissensions, divisions, envy, drunkenness, orgies, and things like these. I warn you, as I warned you before, that those who do such things will not inherit the kingdom of God. But the fruit of the Spirit is love, joy, peace, patience, kindness, goodness, faithfulness, gentleness, self-control. . . . If we live by the Spirit, let us also keep in step with the Spirit" (Gal. 5:19–23, 25).

It is easy to focus on the part of the list mentioning orgies, sorcery, and idolatry and be confident that we don't do those things. However, the list also speaks of hatred, discord, envy, dissensions, and selfish ambition, which are not as easy to dodge.

The fruit of the Spirit is not idealistic poetry, but rather is what happens when Jesus can increase in us as we decrease. Life changes when our actions are accomplished through peace, patience, kindness, goodness, faithfulness, gentleness, and self-control. But what is possible through the Spirit is cut off if we do not decisively deal with the competing desires of our sinful nature.

The fruit of our lives can be very telling. For example, what do you get when you squeeze an orange? Obviously, you get orange juice—what is on the inside. When life squeezes us, what do you get? Hopefully, we give evidence of God's Spirit dwelling within us.

All desires that compete with the kingdom find their source in our innate selfishness. James makes it clear what the source of temptation is when he says, "But each person is tempted when he is lured and enticed by his own desire" (James 1:14). The contrast between our selfishness and godly character makes it easy to spot a weed when we see one.

As followers of Jesus, we must be aware of the seed-sowing machines all around us. Movies, magazines, conversations, lifestyles, and marketing gimmicks constantly bombard us with suggestions that compete with kingdom life. Slick, inviting advertisements continuously seek to persuade us that we must have whatever someone is trying to sell in order to be happy.

If we let these seeds grow, the weeds produced will choke out our desire for the kingdom's way of life. If we let our lives get too acidic by focusing on "me" instead of on Jesus, these competing suggestions will flourish. The promise of pleasure and self-satisfaction is hard to refuse. However, God is calling us to a level of life much higher than selfish pursuits.

Doing Nothing

Grass needs help to grow. Weeds simply need you to do nothing. When you see a field, check to see if the farmer is managing it properly. A field of blue-green grass flowing in the wind doesn't just happen. Someone did something on purpose.

When the land manager is doing nothing, weeds show up and destroy every good intention for a harvest. Weeds bring death. They are great at blocking out the light. Jesus intended for his audience to hear the gravity of his parable lest they become victims of the power of weeds.

The Good Stuff

There's a big difference in food value and protein levels from one type of grass to another. The better grasses, like timothy, orchard grass, and alfalfa, are high in protein but require reseeding to keep them going. We say in the country that the good stuff "plays out," so it must constantly be reseeded. The seed of the kingdom is the Word of God. To make the good grass flourish, we must constantly reseed the soil of our lives with study and meditation on the Word.

In my area, we depend on fescue grass because of its hardiness and ability to survive and keep coming back. One can get by with fescue, but the better grasses produce a better calf crop. Many Christians are not reseeding through personal study of God's Word, and therefore, they are just surviving spiritually. It requires extra effort to have a rich crop of the "good stuff."

Joining a Bible study group, reading in the arenas of church history, apologetics, or philosophy, and reading commentaries and systematic theologies will deepen your appreciation for and involvement in our faith. We have a rich heritage of great thinkers and godly people who offer thought-provoking inquiry into the deeper nuances of the faith. To love God with all of your mind is to explore questions and gain a background understanding of the tenets of our faith that many just memorize without an appreciation for the questions they seek to answer.

When caring for soil, there is more to do than just balance the pH. Nutrients such as potash, nitrogen, and other substances are added to the soil to feed the grass. When compost is prepared for use as a fertilizer, leaves and other organic materials can die and decay to provide food for the plants in our garden. Dying to self is part of the call of the kingdom, and like compost, it feeds life in the kingdom—providing a rich harvest of thirty, sixty, or a hundredfold.

Daily Reminders

When Jesus spoke in parables, he used simple stories taken from life to communicate the truths of the kingdom. Since the parables used everyday images, his audience could be reminded daily of the eternal truths that the parables conveyed.

Every stand of grass or lawn you see can trigger thoughts about your own spiritual battle with weeds. Each field or lawn speaks volumes about its caretaker. If you know a spiritual weed when you see one, you have an advantage. You can cut the weed down to interrupt the seed cycle or dig it out by the roots and then feed the soil. As a result, you will enjoy greater benefits of life in the kingdom. Those who carefully balance their pH and constantly reseed will allow the Word of the kingdom to produce the intended harvest in their lives.

I raise cattle, but in reality, I'm a grass producer. If there is no grass, then there won't be any cattle. Taking it a step further, I'm a weed fighter. If there is going to be any grass for the cows to eat, I must successfully deal with weeds.

To say I'm a follower of Jesus is to say I fight with weeds. The level to which I tend the soil of my life, seed and reseed, and cut down and dig up by the roots every competing desire is the level to which I enjoy life in the kingdom.

Our lives are vivid expressions of whether we are intentional in our desire for the good grass of the kingdom. Remember, doing nothing spiritually assures that weeds will choke out the kingdom grasses. However, by taking purposeful action, you can ensure that the good, nutrient-rich grass of the kingdom grows in your life and provides the life-giving harvest God intended.

A Word of Encouragement

Just as it is important to recognize weeds that compete with growing grass, it is also critical that we identify desires in our lives that compete with God's kingdom.

Is the soil of your life acidic?

What signals in your life tell you that you are out of balance?

In what ways do you reseed and apply fertilizer so the good grass of the kingdom can thrive?

CHAPTER 7

THE KINGDOM OF GOD

The kingdoms of the world expand their borders by force, requiring their captives to submit to a new way of life. God's kingdom is entered willingly by the few who see it as the chance of a lifetime to live under the life-giving rule of God.
—Ed Malone

THERE ARE MORE THAN ONE HUNDRED REFERENCES TO the kingdom of God in the New Testament. Jesus began his public ministry with the words, "Repent, for the kingdom of heaven is at hand" (Matt. 4:17). Jesus taught about the kingdom through parables that compare everyday life to kingdom life. The question of Jesus being a king and having a kingdom was addressed to the end of his life, even in his trial before Pilate.

When Israel refused to listen to the voice of the prophets, they were taken into captivity to Babylon. Prophets such as Ezekiel and Daniel promised a time when the kingdom would be reestablished. Ezekiel 21 declared that the crown would be returned to the One to whom it rightly belonged.

The Jewish people wanted a king in order to do away with Roman control of their nation. Their desire was for independence, military might, and the economic benefits of being a powerful nation. In sharp contrast to their desires, Jesus gave a description of who would be in God's kingdom:

Blessed are the poor in spirit, for theirs is the kingdom of heaven. Blessed are those who mourn, for they shall be comforted. Blessed are the meek, for they shall inherit the earth. Blessed are those who hunger and thirst for righteousness, for they shall be satisfied. Blessed are the merciful, for they shall receive mercy. Blessed are the pure in heart, for they shall see God. Blessed are the peacemakers, for they shall be called sons of God. Blessed are those who are persecuted for righteousness' sake, for theirs is the kingdom of heaven. (Matt. 5:3–10)

It isn't hard to see why this profile of the members of God's kingdom failed to attract those looking for power and political freedom. The meek and poor in spirit recognized their need for God's help. Those who mourn their sinful condition and hunger and thirst for righteousness want their lives to be as God desires. The peacemakers and the merciful know the heart of God, and therefore work for peace and are merciful to others. The pure in heart are single-minded in their desire for God and his kingdom. Those persecuted for righteousness' sake are willing to give whatever is necessary (even life itself) for the cause of the kingdom. The few who enter the kingdom do so in pursuit of God rather than a what's-in-it-for-me motivation.

The warning Jesus gave that the gate is small, the way narrow, and only a few will choose the road of the kingdom is quite sobering. Most folks simply follow accepted patterns of living that they are brought up with or see around them, whereas entrance into the kingdom requires walking a different path through a small gate that does not attract a crowd.

A Treetop Sanctuary

I remember the first time I noticed the small gate and the narrow road of the kingdom. As a young boy, I enjoyed climbing to the top of a big silver-leaf maple tree in our front yard. There I had a private sanctuary and a view that brought my world into a sharp perspective.

From my vantage point, I saw a huge manufacturing plant, our church, the high school, the duck pond (which was a great fishing spot), and the cattle on the farm around my home. As I lay in the branches of my tree, it was fascinating to watch the clouds pass by against the backdrop of an infinite sky.

Everything that came into my view prompted me to ask questions: What does all this mean? How do I fit into the hustle and bustle going on beneath my tree? Do people know where they are going and why? When I looked at the sky in all its wonder, the thought pressed upon me of something existing beyond what I could see. It was an inkling, an idea—the small gate.

People passed beneath my tree, going about their lives. Everything seemed disturbingly orchestrated by directives about how to live and what was important in life. At my age, these markers were loud and clear: sports, girls, and popularity were offered as the golden rings of happiness. In the years ahead, the focus shifted to making all the money you can to accumulating all the stuff you can to being amply prepared for a life of ease in retirement. All of this seemed empty. It certainly failed to match the wonder of what I felt pulling at me from my tree.

The small gate and narrow road represent the drawing of God, which questions our view of life's meaning. When sensitive to it, the awareness of something bigger than life presses upon us. In looking back, it is alarming to consider how easy it could have been to dismiss my treetop experiences. I could have quit asking questions and simply taken life at face value by joining everyone else in the pursuit of all that my natural world had to offer. After all, the promise of fame, pleasure, and fortune is quite attractive. Therefore, it is important to climb high enough in your tree to get away from the noise of the broad highway in order to feel this special drawing of God.

Needing a Shepherd

Entering a kingdom where there is already a king can be risky. How will I fit into this kingdom? What are the benefits and demands?

A king has rules. A kingdom has boundaries. What is the king like? Can he be trusted? What is the purpose of this kingdom?

A few years ago, my wife and I were working at a home for boys. One of these boys and his brother had come to us after spending time living on their own. They had become involved in drugs for self-gratification and as a livelihood. Lacking the judgment needed to make good choices, they had been living in an adult world of crime and pleasure.

On a trip to town for one of the brothers to buy something he had been saving his money to purchase, he told me that he really liked me. I told him it was because he had been able to con me into taking him to town. He said, "No, I like you because you are the one who makes us do what we are supposed to do."

While living with us, he was earning money by working for it. This gave him great satisfaction. The rules governing his new living arrangement demanded mutual respect, proper language, and appropriate response to those in leadership. Because he was learning to follow these rules, he could lie down at night feeling good about himself. This was in great contrast to the fear, greed, and selfishness associated with his former way of life.

He was gaining a positive outlook on who he was becoming. He appreciated the one who made him do what helped him feel good about himself. He was willing to submit to the leadership of one who had his best interests at heart and would help him do what was right by enforcing guidelines and boundaries that would give him a future.

In the same way, the kingdom of God is good news for those desiring to change. It is acknowledging God as the One who will lead as they make choices in life. God's intention is for our good. Jeremiah 29:11, 13 states: "For I know the plans I have for you, declares the Lord, plans for welfare and not for evil, to give you a future and a hope. . . . You will seek me and find me, when you seek me with all your heart."

God could enforce our submission, but he doesn't. We must acknowledge our need for his shepherding. When we recognize God as supreme in value and authority, we can enjoy the life-giving principles of his kingdom. If we do, God is the one helping us to lie down at night feeling good about who he enables us to become.

The Way to Life

At this point, we need to return to the quote from Matthew 5 made at the beginning of this chapter, giving the profile of those in God's kingdom. Jesus said kingdom citizens are meek and poor in spirit, desiring God's shepherding; they mourn their sinful condition, hunger and thirst for righteousness, live as peacemakers, extend mercy to others, are single-minded in their desire for God, and are willing to give whatever is necessary (even life itself) for the cause of the kingdom.

If you count yourself as being in God's kingdom, what is the evidence demonstrating that your pursuit of God matches the description Jesus gave? Do you live in self-sufficiency or God-dependence? Do you have desires for your life that can only be achieved with God's help?

Do you mourn or grieve your sinful condition as compared to God's standard of righteousness? How often do you join Paul in saying, "For I have the desire to do what is right, but not the ability to carry it out. For I do not do the good I want, but the evil I do not want is what I keep on doing. . . . Wretched man that I am! Who will deliver me from this body of death? Thanks be to God through Jesus Christ our Lord!" (Rom. 7:18–19, 24–25).

It is startling to hear Jesus use words such as grieve (emotional pain of the heart) and hunger and thirst (the powerful drives that keep us alive) to describe kingdom citizens. Folks who mourn their sin are quite rare. In fact, most folks have become quite desensitized to sin. The Old Testament prophet Jeremiah challenged Israel's complacency with their sin: "Were they ashamed when they committed abomination? No, . . . they did not know how to blush" (Jer. 6:15). The images and content of the movies and TV shows offered as entertainment are testimonies to humanity's comfortableness with sin. Jesus wept when confronted with the sin of Israel. The intensity of hungering and thirsting for life in the character of God (his righteousness) is an expression also seldom seen among those claiming to be God's people.

Peter writes about hungering and thirsting for God: "Like newborn infants, long for the pure spiritual milk, that by it you may grow up into salvation—if indeed you have tasted that the Lord is good" (1 Pet. 2:2–3).

Peter states that even the smallest encounter with God should produce a hunger for more. For most people, it only takes a taste of something sweet to stir a desire for all they can have. Surely, the same should hold true with God.

Peter's emphasis on craving for the things of God is quite a challenge. Think of pizza, chocolate, or ice cream. The idea of having an intense desire for God is a stretch for those who only go to church to make sure the deal with God about life after death stays paid up.

The concept of hungering for God is illustrated vividly for me when I feed our pets. Cats are frustrating because they might take a hesitant bite or even ignore what I place in front of them, as if offended that there's not something better. On the other hand, feeding my Labrador retriever is a treat. Lady meets me as I'm carrying her food, bouncing all over the place with eager anticipation for whatever is in her bowl. She eats as if I am going to take it back before she is finished or like it's the last meal she'll ever get. It is a genuine pleasure to feed her.

How does God view your spiritual craving for him? Do you take a taste with the tip of your tongue, or do you show up with a huge bowl? Do you seek all you can get? Do you delight in being fed spiritually? As Jesus said, the desire for God in this way is only seen among the few.

The psalmist declared: "As a deer pants for flowing streams, so pants my soul for you, O God. My soul thirsts for God, for the living God" (Ps. 42:1–2). Many in our modern religious culture show up only if they are entertained and not confronted with God through his Word. Self-help and lighthearted preaching are all they will tolerate. Try replacing the entire meeting time with teaching from the Scriptures and see if folks will continue to come. Having a desire for God in the way the psalmist described is not the driving force for those simply attending church events. In fact, many will only come if they can enjoy the hype and glamor of a Hollywood production!

Even a small glimpse of God's plan and purpose for us should stir an excitement to pursue all that is available. Our willingness to be shaped, recreated, and matured in God's righteousness makes our world God's laboratory in which he works with us as his children.

Sadly, many people involved in church are not familiar with or have any desire for the kingdom's way of life. When it comes to their day-to-day activities, there is little difference in how they live as compared to those outside of the church. Most professing Christians blend into our cultural way of life with little distinction.

The first word of the kingdom Jesus spoke was "Repent, for the kingdom of heaven is at hand." The call to repentance is to change, turn around, and go in a different direction. The mindset for many churches is to make those who come feel good, have fun, and enjoy themselves. On the other hand, Jesus was confrontational in his call for change. He demanded that those in God's kingdom no longer live at peace with their culture, pursuing the stuff of this world, but instead be those who hunger and thirst for God and his righteousness. It is clear that Jesus did not embrace the modern methods for drawing a crowd. His call for his followers to deny themselves, take up their cross, and follow him would not fit well among the seeker-friendly approach seen in a lot of churches today.

Personal Inventory

It is important to take a personal inventory when discussing kingdom life. In what ways do you violate the standard of life Jesus lived? Are you personally committed to the kingdom's life-giving ways? Do you have a desire to honor the King of the kingdom?

Maybe we need to be more specific in describing how life in the kingdom works. Did Jesus argue? Was he rude or self-seeking? Did he respond to the needs of others? Did he react to every unfair or unkind statement addressed to him? Was he always sensitive and willing to help those in need?

Living in a Distinct Way

In the Old Testament, the Jews stood out as unique among the nations around them. They spoke Hebrew, circumcised their male children, had rules about what they ate, rested on the Sabbath, served only one God, and didn't use idols in their worship. However, much of their distinction consisted of outward expressions of religious activity that did not keep them centered in the desires God had for them.

Moses expressed the definitive mark of what it meant to belong to God when he prayed, "If your presence will not go with me, do not bring us up from here. For how shall it be known that I have found favor in your sight, I and your people? Is it not in your going with us, so that we are distinct, I and your people, from every other people on the face of the earth?" (Ex. 33:15–16).

Many consider the distinction of being a Christian as going to church. But our true uniqueness as followers of Jesus is evident when he goes with us in our daily living. There is a big difference in visiting Jesus once a week and having him go with you in your daily living. Those who have been truly transformed by God stand out. They are the ones who love their wives as Christ loved the church, who walk in love as Christ loved us, and who bring the light of the kingdom into a world of darkness.

The Model

In Rom. 12:9–18, Paul gives a powerful description of the kingdom way of life:

> Let love be genuine. Abhor what is evil; hold fast to what is good. Love one another with brotherly affection. Outdo one another in showing honor. Do not be slothful in zeal, be fervent in spirit, serve the Lord. Rejoice in hope, be patient in tribulation, be constant in prayer. Contribute to the needs of the saints and seek to show hospitality. Bless

those who persecute you; bless and do not curse them. Rejoice with those who rejoice, weep with those who weep. Live in harmony with one another. Do not be haughty, but associate with the lowly. Never be wise in your own sight. Repay no one evil for evil, but give thought to do what is honorable in the sight of all. If possible, so far as it depends on you, live peaceably with all.

If you make a quick read of this quote from Romans 12, it will fail to impact you as it should. A closer look is important. To abhor evil has been replaced in our society with a call to be tolerant. Evil is wrong. It is an offense to God and robs us of life. To outdo one another in showing honor is a quality rare in our world. Contributing to the needs of the saints and seeking to be hospitable is another virtue quite absent from our modern way of life. Haughtiness and being wise in our own sight are the opposite of being able to be taught or accepting more than one way of doing something. The call of doing what is honorable and promoting peace would certainly heal a lot of wounds in our world. To follow the intention of Romans 12 is to live the way of the kingdom. It is different. It is to repent—to go in a different direction. It is what shapes us, gives us life, and allows others to see the beauty of God.

Grow Up to Salvation

Life in the kingdom is about change as we grow in spiritual maturity. As in life, the journey from childhood to adulthood is difficult. God's desire is for us to grow spiritually, yet he must wait until his desire becomes ours. The apostle Paul presses the importance of making a personal decision to leave our childish ways: "When I was a child, I spoke like a child, I thought like a child, I reasoned like a child. When I became a man, I gave up childish ways" (1 Cor. 13:11). Tragically, many people wait longer than they should to acknowledge the immaturity of their way of life.

Life in God's kingdom is a personal decision not to be ruled by immaturity. For Christians, this means living like Jesus. It is being deliberate rather than impulsive and God-centered rather than me-centered. It is a self-imposed standard of identifying ourselves in Christ.

There are several important activities for citizens of God's kingdom. From a relational standpoint, we seek to make the kingdom visible to others by honoring Jesus in our words and actions. We constantly try to be sensitive to God's gentle prompting as he seeks to express himself through us. Rather than living by the assumed standards of our culture, we look critically at the many automatic actions or activities to which we're accustomed. Instead of reflecting the current fads and trends of our world, we seek to live in the uniqueness of the way Jesus lived.

The New Testament makes a distinction between life in God's kingdom and simply being alive. Just as we have many ways in the English language to describe life, the Greek New Testament uses multiple words when referring to life. One example is the Greek word *bios* from which we get biology.

Zoe, Not Bios

The following example from John 10 demonstrates how the New Testament writers came to reserve the Greek word *zoe* (zo-ay) to refer to the special quality of life Jesus offered. "I came that they may have life (*zoe*) and have it abundantly" (John 10:10). Every human being possesses life, animation, and vitality—*bios*. In Jesus, there is fullness of life—the *zoe* experience of connection with God. It is more than existence. It is found only in God. It is the special, vibrant quality of living in the presence of God.

One final comment needs to be made about the small gate and narrow road. Jesus spoke of there being two roads in life. One leads to destruction and the other to life. To say that one road leads to heaven while the other leads to hell misses an important point Jesus was making. Heaven is a benefit of traveling the narrow road, but is not the destination. Life is not found in a place, but in a person. Jesus taught that the Father has life (*zoe*) in himself (John 5:26). Those entering through the small gate and traveling the narrow road do so in pursuit of God rather than seeking for a what's-in-it-for-me destination. Many want to go to heaven when they die. Unless they are single-minded in their desire for God and his righteousness, they will not be among the few who will enjoy life with God in a place called heaven.

The Sky's the Limit

If the principles of the kingdom become your way of life, Paul's words in Ephesians 3:20–21 will be fulfilled in you: "Now to him who is able to do far more abundantly than all that we ask or think, according to the power at work within us, to him be glory in the church and in Christ Jesus throughout all generations, forever and ever. Amen."

We use the cliché "the sky's the limit" to describe things that have endless possibilities. Paul's statement about God's ability to do more in us than we can ask or imagine certainly sets the stage for an exciting future. When we allow God to work within us, he is glorified, and we experience a quality of life that only a relationship with him can bring.

Over the course of time, there are those who have left the broad path in order to travel the narrow road of the kingdom, but many do not. Recently, something happened on the farm that reminded me of the response many make when God approaches them about entering his kingdom. Sadly, many ignore or even outright reject God's calling to a higher dimension of life.

Going in the Wrong Direction

On this particular day, my border collie, Sada, had been alerting me to the fact that a new calf was bedded down in the woods next to our house. At the end of the day, I went with her to check on it. When I examined the calf, she responded in fear and went running down the hill. At the bottom of the hill, she fled to the backside of the farm. I followed to return her to the field where she could reconnect with her mother. When I entered that field, the calf, much to my amazement, ran through the fence, into the creek, and headed downstream. Once the calf was in the water, I knew she wouldn't be able to find her way back home.

The newborn calf was in quite a dilemma—running from the one who had only good intentions for her. The path she took downstream was leading to her death; however, my approach to her was outside of any comfortable experience in her short life.

Sada and I ran through the woods to get ahead of the calf to turn her back upstream. It was the time of year when a spring-fed creek is very cold, requiring a hearty commitment to enter!

Even with Sada and me in front of her, the calf kept coming downstream rather than turning around. I tackled her and held on while getting my belt off to use as a lead rope to take her home. My attempt to lead her back to the farm was met with bold resistance. Slipping and falling in the creek while dragging a stiff-necked calf was quite the task! She ignored my attempt to tell her she was going in the wrong direction. My warning that she was choosing death by fighting against me was rejected as well.

Finally, we were out of the stream and on our way back to the calf's mother. The three of us crossing the field painted a thought-provoking picture. On my left was Sada, who would follow me off a cliff, and on my right was a calf resisting my effort to give her life. Unlike the calf, my border collie loves and trusts me. I don't need a lead rope for her; I can't get out of her sight, even when I want to! On the other extreme was the calf, resisting my intention to give her life.

Sada and I got mom and calf reunited and made our way back up the hill to the house. Sada was thrilled to have been on another adventure with me, and I was thrilled to experience God speaking to me through an everyday experience, teaching me about his kingdom.

Don't Resist

Many go in the opposite direction from God. Even when we do, he doesn't give up or quit when we go the wrong way. His pursuit of us is driven by his desire to give us life. God wants us to be like Sada—loving and trusting him and feeling thrilled to be with him doing whatever needs to be done. God's ways are like the lead rope I used with the calf. They keep us from going in the direction leading to death. The less we resist by trusting the Shepherd, the easier it is to enjoy the life he's trying to give.

Sada is teaching me how I should behave in the kingdom. It's about walking with God without a lead rope, wanting to be there, and not letting the Shepherd get out of my sight. If Sada could talk, she'd say, "I'd rather be on an adventure with my master than to eat when I'm hungry." For her there are no words more exciting to hear than, "Come! we have things to do!" She doesn't ask why, when we will be back, if she'll miss supper, or if it's going to be hard. At the sound of my voice, her ears stand up, her eyes sparkle, and every fiber of her being responds in joy to the pleasure of hearing my call.

Sada doesn't mind being under my authority. In fact, she thrives on it. She wants to please me and would risk her life to do whatever she thinks I want or need. I can only hope that my desire for God's leadership in my life will one day match Sada's dedication to me. Not all dogs are geared like Sada, just as not all people are willing to respond to God's prompting concerning his kingdom. It's your choice to sit in the recliner with the remote or to always be looking, listening, and waiting for the Master's call to go on a kingdom adventure.

Seeing What Others Pass By

God's kingdom is a special realm in which life is experienced in full by following the will of the Father. Those who see what others pass by make an all-out effort, letting nothing stand in their way to experience the joy of life with God. When all is said and done, *kingdom* is the right word to describe a relationship with God. God is King and he does rule. However, unlike expressions of kingdom in our world, our King died so we can live, and he rules so that we can find life.

A Word of Encouragement

Don't let anything distract you or stand in your way as you diligently pursue the One who touches your life, inviting you to enter by the small gate of his kingdom.

CHAPTER 8

TO YOUR ADVANTAGE

Change is often hard to embrace. When Jesus told his disciples that their relationship to him must move to a spiritual plane rather than him being physically present, they resisted. Accepting this as the better way was outside of their ability to grasp.
—Ed Malone

IT WAS JUST HOURS BEFORE THE CRUCIFIXION. LESS THAN a week had passed since the triumphal entry into Jerusalem. The last few days for Jesus had been extremely intense. The religious leadership was pressing an all-out campaign to destroy him. As a welcomed break from all the conflict, Jesus and his disciples gathered in an upper room for the observance of the annual celebration of Passover. He communicates that the certainty of his death was at hand, and once again, he attempted to help them understand that his death would be within the will of the Father. His words were hard to take in as he spoke; it was to their advantage that he would go to the One who had sent him.

This inner group had left their source of income and families, spending three years traveling throughout Israel with Jesus. They had witnessed healings, people raised from the dead, storms quieted, and crowds fed, and heard him teach with words challenging the soul. The way Jesus lived before them was exemplary as he constantly lifted the bar higher and higher for how to live honorably before the Father. It was beyond their grasp that all of this was about to change. That he was leaving was unthinkable. That it would be better for him to go was incomprehensible. After all, Jesus was thirty-three years old and in the prime of life. He was the one they had been longing for to lead them to the pure ways of God. For the last one thousand days, they had been on a journey with him. It had been the experience of a lifetime.

His disciples begged him not to go. Jesus explained that it was to their advantage that he go so that the Holy Spirit would come. His explanation that his ministry would enlarge greatly through the new age of the Spirit was hard for them to accept. The disciples were not ready to embrace life in the Spirit as better than being with him face to face. Jesus told them that Spirit life gives everyone the opportunity for him to live in them. In this way, his ministry is enlarged to greater dimensions than when he is with them confined in a physical body. They wanted to hold on to what we would prefer for ourselves—God in the flesh living among us. Having Jesus physically present would be easier for them, but would fall short of reaching the need of all humanity.

God is Spirit. Through a spiritual relationship with him, God is calling us to a higher plane—life in God's realm. We want to bring God down to us, while God wants to bring us up to him. What God calls us to is better for us and all of humanity.

For the disciples, life with Jesus changed dramatically after his death and resurrection. How to magnify their spiritual sensitivity for this new approach to work pressed upon them. Questions swirled as to how to live in this new age of the Spirit. It was not as if they knew nothing about being spiritually in touch with the Father. They had been led by the Spirit to John the Baptist and then to Jesus. By maturing in their ability to live in the realm of the Spirit, life would be taken to a higher plane.

We are a composite of body, soul, mind, and spirit. We are more than the body we live in. Through self-reflection, the moral press of conscience, and the capacity to love, we function on a deeper side of life. The disciples' task was to deepen their spiritual capacity that was already a part of their lives.

Miracle of Our World

The starting point for a spiritual relationship with God begins with the awareness of his presence. The apostle Paul states, "For what can be known about God is plain to them, because God has shown it to them. For his invisible attributes, namely, his eternal power and divine nature, have been clearly perceived, ever since the creation of the world, in the things that have been made. So they are without excuse" (Rom. 1:19–20).

Observing the majesty and grandeur of life allows us to see the fingerprint of God on the things he has made. Each occasion of searching to understand things like the miracle of sight, the wonder of our thought processes, and the marvelous inner workings of a cell provides the setting for an epiphany with God.

The more you look, the more of God you see. Contact with God in this way strengthens our sensitivity to his presence as we stand with him observing his handiwork. Continual experiences with God and worshiping him as our Creator help us discern his presence.

Much in life is observed without appreciating the magnitude of what is going on. Noticing what others fail to see provides an encounter with our God. For example, when a tree puts forth its leaves in the spring, very few are taken back in awe. For them, it is a mundane, annual occurrence. A closer look is mind-blowing and brings one into the presence of God.

Chad's Epiphany

I remember one Sunday morning when Chad, my racquetball partner and best friend, came to church all excited. The fact that Chad was excited was normal. As a seeker of God, he was always thinking and couldn't wait to share his experiences. We listened as he spoke of his epiphany with God. Keeping up with his thinking was, at times, a strain. When he spoke, his eyes would light up, his charming smile would draw you in, and his enthusiasm would hold you on the edge of his every word.

"It is an explosion!" he explained. "A mature oak tree produces two hundred thousand leaves in a span of days. A plant cell is only ten microns in diameter. It takes one hundred thousand cells lined up, side by side, to span one inch." He paused for a moment, allowing us to catch up with him. "Can you wrap your mind around how many cell divisions per second are needed to grow this many leaves in one tree?" The answer approaches several million cell divisions per second—a process lasting for several days.

At this point, Chad rejoined the enthusiasm he experienced when first considering this concept. With a radiating smile and all the intensity he could express, he said, "It is an explosion! All of this activity started with a single cell division in each leaf. The process builds in momentum like a train racing down the track." With a startling look of amazement on his face, he said, "While progressing at full speed, all of a sudden the whole process stops. Each leaf, several cell levels thick, is perfectly formed and spaced on the tree in a way to maximize photosynthesis. The tree brings forth its leaves at the right time, producing not too many or too few." No one spoke.

Chad led us into the presence of God through his excitement and praise for our Creator. He had an epiphany with God because he had eyes with which to see. Chad's deeper look into the miracle of life drew him into a place where God met him. Meeting God by exploring the wonder of his world enlarges our awareness of the spiritual dimension of life.

Spiritual awareness of God is also prompted when we step aside from the hustle and bustle of life, being still, meditating, and asking meaning-of-life questions. For many, standing in front of a waterfall or a breathtaking sunset or being enraptured by the sound of a gently flowing stream pulls them into the deeper side of life. For others, sitting under the night sky gives perspective to our insignificance and presses us to know what lies beyond. Seeing without eyes, hearing without ears, and feeling without hands draws us closer into God's realm. Self-reflection and response to the inner moral press take us before the Father in spiritual accountability.

Some stop and smell the flowers, while others race by. There are many opportunities to be drawn into God's spiritual realm. For example, Moses was on Mount Horeb tending sheep when he came upon a bush that was burning. A bush on fire was not unusual. Practical explanations, such as a lightning strike or an animal slipping on a piece of flint and causing a spark, could create the fire. Instead of dismissing this event with surface explanations, Moses noticed something deeper going on—the bush was not being consumed by the fire. "And Moses said, 'I will turn aside to see this great sight, why the bush is not burned.' When the LORD saw that he turned aside to see, God called to him out of the bush, 'Moses, Moses!' And he said, 'Here I am'" (Ex. 3:3–4). It was only when Moses asked why the bush was not being consumed that God met him at that moment. One can only wonder how often we fail to hear from God because we do not stop to look more deeply. Inner thoughts that press upon us should not be dismissed easily. Every curious thought is not from God—but some are. Thoughts wrapped in God's presence should stand out boldly to those who make a practice of meeting with God while observing the wonder of his creation.

The powerful result of staying sensitive to God's presence cannot be overstated. At a very early age, we become aware of God's presence as he confronts us at the level of conscience. Living in a permissive culture desensitizes our conscience. If we are not being confronted with the Scriptures, we can easily blend into the way of life around us and ignore the press from God.

Sensing God's presence by being in a personal relationship with him provides a monitor for when we are not going in the right direction or are neglecting things that matter to him. Just as we experience in our relationships with others, we can sense when things are not right when the bond of fellowship with God is broken. There are numerous indicators to alert us to this break in relationship before words are even spoken. Scripture calls for us to not grieve the Spirit within us. When our fellowship with God is broken, he grieves the loss. If our love for God is strong and we want to please him, his displeasure because of our sin confronts us.

Practice the Presence

The Practice of the Presence of God by Brother Lawrence was written more than three hundred years ago. Through three centuries, the devotion of Brother Lawrence has encouraged many in the pursuit of God's presence. Brother Lawrence disciplined himself to stay aware of God in all circumstances. As a servant of Jesus, he speaks of feeling closer to God when washing the pots and pans than when participating in Holy Communion.

Many of us have times when we sense God's presence, yet before we realize it, we are busily going about our lives unaware of God. It is nice to have the occasion to pull away and sit by the creek and enjoy God's presence. However, we cannot live at the creek. There is work to be done. There are responsibilities of family and work taking place in an environment full of noise and stress. Paul offers help for not losing touch with God, regardless of where we are and what is going on: "And whatever you do, in word or deed, do everything in the name of the Lord Jesus, giving thanks to the Father through him. . . . Whatever you do, work heartily, as for the Lord and not for men" (Col. 3:17, 23). Doing something in the name of Jesus is to do it in the character of Jesus, bringing honor to him as the one we follow. This is captured in his teaching, "As you did it to one of the least of these my brothers, you did it to me" (Matt. 25:40).

Therefore, whether it is cooking a meal, changing a diaper, working your job, or being a good neighbor, do it in the character of Christ, as if serving him. We do not have to live by the creek or in a monastery to stay aware of God. Life is not to be divided between the sacred and the mundane. Living by this standard allows us to stay in touch with God, no matter where we are or what we are doing.

Relationships

Relationships vividly portray the spiritual component of life. When you meet someone you know, one you have laughed and cried with, shared hopes and dreams and walked through hard times with, you are quickly aware of whether all is well. Before words are exchanged, spirits connect. Soul mates communicate at a level deeper than words.

Conversations start with the simple exchange of words, yet as the conversation deepens, each person's spirit moves outside of the physical expression of their body, filling the space around them. When this happens, the moment is special as it transcends our physical surroundings. Moving beyond the exchange of thought processes to this type of union doesn't just happen. Getting to a spiritual level in a relationship takes time and desire. Experiencing relationships soul to soul prepares us for relating to God.

The failure of those around Jesus to be in a proper spiritual relationship with the Father cost him his life. God's attempt to validate his Son in their inner spirit was ignored. They were not sensitive to or trained to recognize God's press on their lives. Tragically, many of those rejecting Jesus believed in God, attended temple, and prayed, yet were not spiritually prepared to respond to his Son.

An illustration of living life on the surface and not being aware of the true meaning of life is found in the book of Genesis. The story is of Jacob fleeing from his brother in fear for his life. Jacob tricked his father into giving him the family blessing that belonged to Esau, and now his brother sought to kill him. Fleeing his home in fear, Jacob had a dream in which he saw angels ascending and descending from heaven on a ladder. "Then Jacob awoke from his sleep and said, 'Surely the LORD is in this place, and I did not know it.' . . . How awesome is this place! This is none other than the house of God, and this is the gate of heaven" (Gen. 28:16–17). Jacob's discovery is God's goal for everyone. God desires us to realize that the very world we live in is indeed the gateway to heaven and that he is in this place!

When was the last time you pondered meaning-of-life questions or were drawn by conscience into the throne room of God? Has there been time for meditating, being still, reflecting before the night sky, or meeting God in his world? Through spiritual sensitivity, life takes on a whole new meaning.

Seek and Find God

To clarify the call of following Jesus in a spiritual relationship, we look to an event in the life of the apostle Paul. He was in Athens, Greece, at a place called the Areopagus. Stoic and Epicurean philosophers were among those gathered to discuss the newest things being said about life. When given the opportunity to speak, Paul tells them that it was God who made the world and "that they should seek God, and perhaps feel their way toward him and find him. Yet he is not actually far from each one of us, for 'In him we live and move and have our being'" (Acts 17:27–28).

Seeking and feeling after God is achieved by participating in the spiritual realm. When looking for something, it is important to move in the right direction. One goes to the woods in pursuit of a deer, a mountain stream for trout, or the ocean for a dolphin. God is Spirit; therefore, we must move beyond the surface of life to find God. Seeking implies the requirement of effort and desire in finding what we are looking for. Slipping on a rock and falling into the water is not how one enters the kingdom of God.

The expression *feeling after God* generates the picture of one searching without the ability to see clearly. Like the blind person feeling with their hands in the absence of physical eyesight, finding God requires feeling after God by means other than our natural abilities of sight and sound.

In relationships, we know things without words being spoken. As we mature in life, intuition sharpens our knowledge of things without concrete data. Self-reflection, meditation, and pursuit of the meaning of life allow us to know things in ways that are different and deeper than empirical data. The combined phrase of seeking and feeling after God is a pathway for those who understand life to be composed of more than their physical surroundings.

Paul is quick to say that searching for God is not a hopeless task or out of reach. Rather, God is not far from us. In him we live and have our being. God has not placed us here to watch us fail in our pursuit of him, but he readily meets those who diligently seek after him. The result of our seeking is knowing (experiencing) God—a treasured blessing. Jesus, in the Sermon on the Mount, said, "Ask, and it will be given to you; seek, and you will find; knock, and it will be opened to you" (Matt. 7:7). To ask, seek, and knock is to pursue God with increasing diligence.

What substantiates our diligent seeking after God? Listening to a pastor preach every week hardly qualifies as an effort on our part to know God more deeply. In today's sound-bite culture, keeping the attention of churchgoers for more than twenty minutes of teaching is a monumental task. Why is this so? The same audience will sit for two hours in a theater mesmerized by the current movie production. Watching sporting events for hours is equally no problem. Why is our attention span so short when it comes to the Word? Folks reading a mystery or romance novel are hardly able to lay it down, yet cannot make it through one chapter in the Scriptures without losing focus and the desire to continue.

Before drawing this chapter to a close, it is important to focus our attention once again on Jesus telling the disciples that it was necessary for him to go back to the Father to set free the new age of the Spirit. Understandably, the disciples wanted to hold on to the way things had been. However, God, in Christ, was doing something much larger than they could imagine.

A Promise Fulfilled

When Jesus spoke of life in the Spirit, he was announcing the fulfillment of promises God gave in the Old Testament. By his life, death, and resurrection, Jesus brought into being the new age of the Spirit:

> For this is the covenant I will make with the house of Israel after those days, declares the LORD: I will put my law within them, and I will write it on their hearts. And I will be their God, and they shall be my people. And no longer shall each one teach his neighbor and each his brother, saying, "Know

the LORD," for they shall all know me, from the least of them to the greatest, declares the LORD. (Jer. 31:33–34)

And it shall come to pass afterward, that I will pour out my Spirit on all flesh; your sons and your daughters shall prophesy, your old men shall dream dreams, and your young men shall see visions. Even on the male and female servants in those days I will pour out my Spirit. (Joel 2:28–29)

And I will give you a new heart, and a new spirit I will put within you. (Ezek. 36:26)

The New Testament presents life in the Spirit as being for all followers of Jesus. The following citations point to the opportunity Jesus gave for everyone to live in this supernatural way of life. It is God's great desire for his people:

I have been crucified with Christ. It is no longer I who live, but Christ who lives in me. (Gal. 2:20)

But I say, walk by the Spirit, and you will not gratify the desires of the flesh. (Gal. 5:16)

If by the Spirit you put to death the deeds of the body, you will live. For all who are led by the Spirit of God are sons of God. (Rom. 8:13–14)

Therefore, if anyone is in Christ, he is a new creation. (2 Cor. 5:17)

To them God chose to make known how great among the Gentiles are the riches of the glory of this mystery, which is Christ in you, the hope of glory. Him we proclaim, warning everyone and teaching everyone with all wisdom, that we may present everyone mature in Christ. (Col. 1:27–28)

His Project or Ours

Jesus was calling the disciples to God's great plan, which began before the world was created. Once we grasp God's purpose and our part in it, maybe ballgames and movies won't have such a hold on us. Possibly, participation in God's project will take precedence over the things that so easily capture our attention, time, and interest.

A cursory outline of the book of Ephesians highlights the plan we can be part of. The scope of this plan is immeasurable. God's goal is to unite all things in Christ, both in heaven and on the earth. What he wants to achieve is possible only if we rise to the level of life in the Spirit:

> In him we have redemption through his blood, the forgiveness of our trespasses, according to the riches of his grace, which he lavished upon us, in all wisdom and insight making known to us the mystery of his will, according to his purpose, which he set forth in Christ as a plan for the fullness of time, to unite all things in him, things in heaven and things on earth. (Eph. 1:7–10)

> For we are his workmanship, created in Christ Jesus for good works, which God prepared beforehand, that we should walk in them. (Eph. 2:10)

> . . . so that through the church the manifold wisdom of God might now be made known to the rulers and authorities in the heavenly places. (Eph. 3:10)

> . . . until we all attain to the unity of the faith and of the knowledge of the Son of God, to mature manhood, to the measure of the stature of the fullness of Christ. (Eph. 4:13)

> Walk as children of the light, . . . and try to discern what is pleasing to the Lord. (Eph. 5:8, 10)

> Finally, be strong in the Lord and in the strength of his might. Put on the whole armor of God, that you may be able to stand against the schemes of the devil. For we do not wrestle against flesh and blood, but against the rulers, against the authorities, against the cosmic powers over this present darkness, against the spiritual forces of evil in the heavenly places. (Eph. 6:10–12)

A Cosmic Salvation

God's plan was formulated before He laid the foundation of the earth. It was designed to reconcile all things in heaven and earth through Jesus. Each of us is part of this plan because God has purposed beforehand good works for us to walk in. As the interconnected body of Christ, we are now on display to the powers in the heavenly places. By the power of the Holy Spirit, we are new creations being transformed and matured into the likeness of Christ as we yield to the will of the Father. We are children of light making it our aim to please him, even when it means that we live in a war zone. It is a battle that is not just against flesh and blood, but is also against cosmic powers seeking to nullify God's plan. What God desires is accomplished by those willing to join forces in bringing glory to God in the midst of a universe having conflicting forces at play. Peter, in his first epistle, speaks of the eagerness of the angels to look into the things God is doing in our world. These Scripture verses from Ephesians speak of the church being an object lesson to the cosmic powers and revealing God's manifold wisdom. Wow! God's plan is cosmic in scale. Isn't it sad that some have reduced his plan to simply an all-about-me salvation?

A Word of Encouragement

When Jesus ascended back to the Father, the Holy Spirit came. Life in the Spirit was no longer a thing hoped for, but it became a present reality. The mission set in front of us is to honor God by being a part of his plan to witness to our world and cosmic powers. Only if we are empowered spiritually as new creations will we fulfill the desires God has for us.

CHAPTER 9

HOW DOES IT WORK?

Explaining how life in the Spirit works was not easy. Using analogous language, Jesus spoke of being born again, sheep hearing the voice of the shepherd, a branch abiding in the vine, and the Holy Spirit as teacher and guide. In this new way of living, sensing and feeling takes precedence over hearing and seeing as the followers of Jesus learn to feel his guidance as it comes wrapped in his presence.
—Ed Malone

JESUS FACED AN ENORMOUS CHALLENGE WHEN HE pointed his followers to life in the Spirit. Following Jesus spiritually presented prodigious questions for the disciples. Their maturing into this new way of living serves as a guide for our journey. Throughout the Gospels and the subsequent writings of the New Testament, pointers for how life in the Spirit works are given.

Ask someone you know who demonstrates maturity in following Jesus to describe what it is like to be in a spiritual relationship with him. Those mature in Spirit life will be cautious when answering your questions. They are quick to admit that their words fall short in capturing how God guides our lives. Feeling the press of God as he touches us is a time to kneel and yield, not a time for capturing in words the nature of what is going on. Experiencing Jesus spiritually is hard to describe, but is undeniable as he empowers our desire to follow him.

The strain of trying to explain certain things falls into the category of tacit knowledge. It is like trying to tell someone how to keep their balance on a bicycle, or like grandma's recipe when she tells you to work the dough until it feels right. Life in the Spirit depends on *feel,* which is spiritually based. The ability to live in a spiritual relationship with Jesus is a continuous pursuit—not a destination. It is a process involving effort and even trial and error.

A Battle

It is important to know that participation in Spirit life is a battle. The spiritual realm is not a neutral arena. Opening yourself to God's Spirit allows an opportunity for the devil, a spiritual being, to create confusion and misdirection. It is easy to think that God has spoken when he hasn't.

False prophets were common during the period of the Old Testament: "I did not send the prophets, yet they ran; I did not speak to them, yet they prophesied" (Jer. 23:21). New Testament believers encountered the same issue as they attempted to walk in Spirit life. John the elder told those around him, "Beloved, do not believe every spirit, but test the spirits to see whether they are from God, for many false prophets have gone out into the world" (1 John 4:1). The apostle Paul warned the Corinthians, "For even Satan disguises himself as an angel of light" (2 Cor. 11:14). Additionally, Paul said to Timothy, "Now the Spirit expressly says that in later times some will depart from the faith by devoting themselves to deceitful spirits and teachings of demons, through the insincerity of liars whose consciences are seared" (1 Tim. 4:1–2).

There is not only a conflict with spirits outside of us, but also within: "For the desires of the flesh are against the Spirit, and the desires of the Spirit are against the flesh, for these are opposed to each other, to keep you from doing the things you want to do" (Gal. 5:17). We are born with an innate selfish spirit that constantly interferes with the desire of the Holy Spirit.

How God Speaks

Another aspect of Spirit life is that God speaks in a variety of ways. Elijah the prophet heard a still, small voice. Jeremiah spoke of

God's Word as being like a hammer or a fire. Dreams were often a medium for the voice of God among many of the prophets. It requires discernment to know whether a thought is from one's mind, the devil, or God. When Moses asked for certainty that it was God speaking to him at the burning bush, he was told that when he got back to this mountain with the people of God, then he would know it was God who had sent him. Moses moved forward in faith, and he later had the validation of what he believed to be true. Looking back sometimes reveals the hand of God, and at other times it reveals our initiative.

There are times when God uses the words of another person to speak to us. When we hear them speak, confirmation of their words being from God is made in our spirit. The person speaking is not aware of the power of their words.

Moses was looking for a lost sheep when he encountered a bush on fire, resulting in an occasion for God to speak to him. The great Christian writer C. S. Lewis said that God's Word often came to him obliquely. When he least expected it, he would have something register with him that he believed to be from God.

The variety of ways in which God speaks and the confusion orchestrated by the devil make it likely that we will make mistakes in discerning the spirit confronting us. Hebrews 5:14 says, "But solid food is for the mature, for those who have their powers of discernment trained by constant practice to distinguish good from evil." Constant practice means we are learning how to do something, yet never master the endeavor. It is like shooting a basketball or hitting a golf ball. It takes practice to do it well and to maintain it. Unless one is honest as to making mistakes while pursuing life in the Spirit, moving to maturity is stalled.

Which Way to Go?

Most people would regard the apostle Paul as one who was mature in Spirit life. Acts 16 picks up on his second missionary journey. Paul thought he and Silas should go to Asia, but was forbidden by the Holy Spirit. His next choice was to go to Bithynia. Again, the

Spirit of Jesus did not allow them. When they arrived in Troas, Paul had a vision in the night to go to Macedonia. Once in Macedonia, they went to Philippi, where he and Silas were beaten and put in jail.

Several questions emerge from these events. Why did Paul, a veteran of Spirit life, have such a hard time figuring out where to go? What was preventing their journey into Asia and then later into Bithynia? Does being jailed in Philippi mean they missed God's direction a third time? Paul and Silas seemed to be comfortable with what happened since they were heard singing praises to God at the midnight hour in their jail cell.

Paul's intention to go to Asia led him through a process of events that took him to Macedonia. The struggle Paul went through in knowing God's will is quite common. Unlike Paul, many within the modern expression of Christianity falsely claim to always know God's leading. Even the great prophet Elijah was confronted with going where God had not led him. The word from God to Elijah as he hid in a cave from Jezebel was, "What are you doing here, Elijah?" (1 Kings 19:9).

An earlier episode recorded in Acts 9 stands in stark contrast to Paul's experience of being led to Macedonia. On the road to Damascus, Paul was blinded by a light as Jesus spoke to him. He was led into the city, where Ananias was called upon to help Paul. "And the Lord said to him, 'Rise and go to the street called Straight, and at the house of Judas look for a man of Tarsus named Saul, for behold, he is praying'" (Acts 9:11). The word from God was specific. Ananias would not be fumbling around in the dark. These two events reveal there are times when God's leading is clear and times when it is difficult to discern.

Another illustration of the challenge of Spirit life is demonstrated when Peter identified Jesus as the Messiah. In Matthew 16, Jesus tells Peter he had reached the correct understanding about him because he had been taught by the Father. Yet when Jesus announced that as Messiah he would die, Peter rebuked him. Jesus told Peter that he had now set his mind on the things of men. Hearing correctly at one point and then drawing his conclusion about what it meant put Peter in a position of standing in the way of what God was doing. This is a common error among the people of God.

Spirit life casts us into a battle that requires maturity gained through practice, and it demands that we discern God's voice in a variety of ways. All of this means that we have a lot to learn. It is essential that we pay close attention to the teaching Jesus gave about life in the Spirit.

Born Again

Jesus told Nicodemus in John 3 that everything begins with being born again. The birth analogy is powerful. As paralleled in the physical, there are spiritual potentials that can be developed or left untouched. The community of believers is a great help for those growing in the Spirit. Observing individuals exhibiting maturity in Spirit life presents a picture of what is possible. The phrase "It takes a village to raise a child" applies to Spirit life as well.

No one envisions a newborn remaining in the crib. From the very first, there are hopes and dreams for a full future. Family comes alongside, encouraging the child to stand, talk, and grow, moving toward maturity. One's church family fulfills this role for the new believer. Jesus presented, in this birth analogy, an endless source of inspiration to those meditating on the parallels between physical and spiritual growth.

The response Nicodemus made to entering his mother's womb a second time indicated that he had many questions about this strange concept. How does it happen? In what way can the infinite God be present in a person?

In describing the meaning of being born again, Jesus said, "The wind blows where it wishes, and you hear its sound, but you do not know where it comes from or where it goes. So it is with everyone who is born of the Spirit" (John 3:8).

There is no easy explanation of the miracle of God indwelling us. We should never cease to be amazed by God's willingness to share life with us in this way. Every moment of life after being born again is a miracle. Understanding and benefiting fully from being born again is an ongoing process.

We experience the wind as the gentle, life-sustaining air we breathe and at other times with a force so strong as to knock down most anything in its path. The wind cannot be controlled, yet its power can be harnessed to move ships and turn turbines to generate power.

Sheep and Shepherd

In John 10, Jesus introduced the analogy of sheep with a shepherd, which spoke loudly to his audience. Their world was one where animals were essential to life. They had personal experience of animals bonding with them as shepherds.

For the past twenty-five years, our family has been blessed with the opportunity of raising Black Angus cattle. As a herdsman, this sheep and shepherd analogy confronts me every day. My cattle know me. They recognize the sound of my voice. They know me as the one bringing hay in the winter and the one moving them from field to field in the summer for better grazing. When I step into the field, they stop grazing and raise their heads, looking my way. They wait for my call and eagerly respond, following me to the next field. I do not have to drive them—they follow. The young calves are different. They do not have experience with me as their herdsman. My wife and our border collie walk behind the calves, encouraging them to follow their mamas.

When Jesus approaches us in the field of our lives, do we quit what we are doing and raise our heads to see if he will call? Do we have any willingness to be shepherded?

Without cattle constantly looking for fresh grass, I would have little opportunity to take them to something better. "Like newborn infants, long for the pure spiritual milk, that by it you may grow up into salvation—if indeed you have tasted that the Lord is good" (1 Pet. 2:2–3). Without a spiritual longing, we cannot be led into green pastures and beside the still waters of God's kingdom. Without having tasted that the Lord is good, we will not desire more of the things of God.

Sadly, many people have no desire for a shepherd. They believe they can do just fine without supervision and guidance. Cattle sure feel that way! That is one reason why we have fences. If left to themselves, cattle will eat their winter supply of hay. Hopefully, we are smarter than cows. However, Isaiah 1:3 states, "The ox knows its owner, and the donkey its master's crib, but Israel does not know, my people do not understand."

Vine and Branch

As a further example of life in the Spirit, Jesus gave the analogy of the vine and branches. Just as the sheep and shepherd analogy resonated well with his audience, so did his reference to grapevines. Everyone was familiar with this staple in Israel's culture.

"I am the true vine, and my Father is the vinedresser. Every branch in me that does not bear fruit he takes away, and every branch that does bear fruit he prunes, that it may bear more fruit. . . . As the branch cannot bear fruit by itself, unless it abides in the vine, neither can you, unless you abide in me. I am the vine; you are the branches. Whoever abides in me and I in him, he it is that bears much fruit, for apart from me you can do nothing" (John 15:1–2, 4–5).

The basic horticultural principle is that branches allow for sap to flow from the vine to feed the leaves, blooms, and fruit. The branch serves as a conduit. If the branch doesn't stay connected, the sap cannot flow and fruit is cut off. A branch left to survive on its own has no chance of fruit. The vinedresser prunes, works against diseases, feeds the vine, and balances the amount of water needed for good fruit production.

The work of the vinedresser (viticulturist) is critical. There are college degree programs in viticulture. The difference between grape jelly and a bottle of wine commanding big dollars is a wide field of applied knowledge.

With Jesus as the Vine and the Father as the Vinedresser, quality fruit can be produced. The whole point of having a grapevine is fruit. In Galatians 5, Paul defines the fruit of the Spirit being love, joy, peace, patience, kindness, goodness, faithfulness, gentleness, and self-control. These qualities are representative of the character of Jesus to be expressed through us.

In Isaiah 5, God spoke of planting choice vines and doing all that was necessary for a harvest, but the result was only wild grapes. Israel was unwilling to cooperate with God for his purposes. Many professing Christians have no concern for fruit production, which brings glory to God. All they are interested in is a safe place to be when this life is over.

Jesus strongly emphasized the union of the vine and branch. On again and off again renders fruit production impossible. Therefore, continuously abiding in mystical union with Christ became a dominant theme in the New Testament.

The apostle Paul wrote in Romans 6:13, "Do not present your members to sin as instruments for unrighteousness, but present yourselves to God as those who have been brought from death to life, and your members to God as instruments for righteousness." Allowing the Spirit of God rather than our selfish spirit to flow through us is the goal. Paul declared in Galatians 5 that there is a war between the desires of the flesh and the Spirit. Learning how to shut off our selfish spirit and allow the Holy Spirit to flow in us is the core of Spirit life.

The ability to be responsive to God requires desire and discipline. When it happens, we are the first to stand in awe. Fruit-of-the-Spirit responses by God flowing through us are miracles.

To Us, Within Us, Through Us

In the born-again analogy, something happens *to* us. In the sheep and shepherd analogy, the ability to follow Jesus is developed *within* us. In the vine and branch analogy, something happens *through* us. The combination of these word pictures points to a new level of supernatural living.

Jesus assured the disciples that when he went away, he would send the Holy Spirit—the Comforter, the Spirit of Truth, the Helper, the One who comes alongside. By building upon the experience of the new birth, we sharpen our awareness of God's presence. As the

Spirit works within us, we can sense that which is holy pressing upon us. Whether in a season of needed comfort or guidance, we can look to God's Spirit for help.

Jesus outlined the work of the Holy Spirit as one who helps, counsels, convicts, guides, teaches, reminds, and glorifies Jesus. He told the disciples that there was much more for them to learn. He said they would not be able to bear the teaching then, but when the Holy Spirit came, he would guide them into all truth. The list of workings of the Holy Spirit is quite broad. The scope of his activity of being our Helper, Comforter, Guide, and Teacher requires a learning process, and therefore is seldom tapped into.

The Power of the Spirit

Having God's Spirit in us is one thing; knowing how to engage the power of the Spirit is another. Visualizing how this works is important. A mental picture stimulates our ability to think through the process. Romans 8 calls for us to walk by the Spirit and to put to death the deeds of the body by the Spirit. The Spirit is the means and power to accomplish the goal identified. How to engage the help of the Spirit in our lives is the question in front of us.

The power of the Spirit working through our lives does not happen unless we take the appropriate action to yield the right-of-way to the Spirit. Many things come together to enable our ability to live by the power of the Spirit. How the indwelling Spirit of God helps us is demonstrated in the following example.

In Luke 6, Jesus instructed his followers to love not as the world does, but to love without expectation of return. Even if we try hard to meet this challenge, we fail. Our greatest desire to love in this way falls short. Loving without expectation is what God does. Being spiritually empowered to love in this way is liberating and uplifting. The Spirit is not a spectator in the stands cheering us on as we give all we have to accomplish the goal. By yielding to the Holy Spirit, something happens beyond our human limitation. Loving without expectation of return happens when the Holy Spirit is allowed to flow through us. It is the result of yielding to the Spirit.

A Second Look

Jesus did not give complete teaching about Spirit life until the end of his ministry. His disciples refused to accept that he was soon to die. It was in the days before his arrest that he taught at length about how life in the Spirit works. With this new understanding, the disciples needed to take a second look at what Jesus had been teaching. Having this added power of the Spirit made a huge difference in how to approach what he had taught them.

The parable of the good Samaritan (Luke 10) calls for loving our neighbor as ourselves. Following the intention of this teaching requires the sensitivity to notice the need, the compassion to not walk by, and the ability to focus on others rather than ourselves.

By spending time with Jesus, we learn to be sensitive to his gentle nudge. When a need is present, his prompting is hard to ignore. Being aware of the presence of the Father in us stimulates our compassion to not walk by. Through the Spirit's ability to teach us, we can seek guidance for how to respond in a way that helps rather than enables. During this process, something special transpires. Those in need receive what they need most—the touch of God. Additionally, we experience the joy of working together with the Spirit in bringing glory to God. This happens only if we are sensitive to God's presence and willingly make the choice to yield.

Heart Sins

As part of the Sermon on the Mount (Matt. 5–7), Jesus spoke of keeping the Ten Commandments. In addressing the commands to not kill or commit adultery, Jesus extended these commands to their root origin—anger and lust. When anger and lust are not shut off, they grow. This growth, if unchecked, leads to the ultimate point of murder and adultery. James teaches that temptation to sin comes by being lured and enticed by our own desire: "Then desire when it has conceived gives birth to sin, and sin when it is fully grown brings forth death" (James 1:15).

Dealing with lust and anger at the level of the heart is to engage the battle of taking every thought captive to obey Christ. Battles with our inner thoughts can linger longer than they should. Some battles are not easily won. The presence of God within us comes to our aid. With the Spirit in us, we should immediately be aware that he is grieved by our state of mind. If God's pleasure matters to us, our feeling of anger or lust will be quickly brought under control to restore peace in our hearts. While in a state of sin, fellowship with God is lost. Sensing the change in fellowship with God should be so striking that it gets our attention. In Colossians 3:15, Paul wrote, "And let the peace of Christ rule in your hearts."

Letting peace rule means that peace is in charge. Christ's peace ruling within us functions like an umpire in football. During a game, the umpire blows a whistle when there is a violation of the rules. Everything stops and is regrouped before play begins again. When peace with God is disrupted by sins of the heart, it should be as if a whistle is blown announcing a foul. If we seldom think about God and don't stay aware of his presence, disruption of fellowship is hardly noticed. To do so allows us to harbor attitudes and passions long enough that we express them. Continual fellowship with God's presence protects us at the root cause of sin—bad desires and thoughts. Unless we act at the beginning of the process of sin, our thoughts are eventually expressed in doing something stupid and/or hurtful.

We can be aware of God by using every avenue available to stay in touch with him. Every opportunity of seeing his fingerprint on the design of life confronts us with God in his awesomeness. At the level of conscience, we are aware of God's authority by sensing something outside of us pressing us to a moral standard. Additionally, the Scriptures provide another way to connect with God. In that the Scriptures are inspired by God, his presence comes across as we read the Word. Multiple arenas of experiencing God are available, yet many people have no interest in using them to stay in touch with him.

One with Our Sin

Shamefully, we bring the Holy Spirit into offensive situations. The apostle Paul admonished the Corinthians for their cultural practice of participating with prostitutes (1 Cor. 6). Paul was horrified that, as followers of Christ, they were bringing Christ into their sin. We, too, should be ashamed when we give the Holy Spirit a front-row seat to the expression of our anger or any other inappropriate emotion or action.

Many go about their lives with little regard for how the Spirit feels about what they are doing. Think about it for a moment. The Holy Spirit, by living in us, has a lot to put up with to be available to help us. Ordinarily, with an important guest in our home, we try to be on our best behavior, yet with the Spirit of the Father at home in us, we do not offer him the same courtesy. The fact that we disregard God's Spirit in this way is atrocious. Does it mean that we don't believe that the Spirit dwells in us or that we don't care how the Spirit feels about what we are doing? Does it mean that the Spirit is not in us even though we profess that he is? Practicing the discipline of staying aware of God's presence and not wanting to grieve him becomes a great weapon to protect us from sin as it originates in the heart.

Being Taught

In John 14–16, Jesus identifies the Holy Spirit as a comforter, guide, and teacher. Learning to be taught by the Holy Spirit adds to spiritual empowerment. Exposure to the Holy Spirit stimulates a new way of thinking and reacting to life.

If we study the teaching of Jesus long enough, our minds pick up his way of thinking. People who saturate themselves in movies often express themselves with memorable phrases they have heard. The goal of followers of Jesus is to be absorbed in his teaching, to think and express ourselves as he did, and to live as he lived.

Followers of Jesus should be constantly reviewing his life and teaching. For example, meditating on the phrase "Do unto others as you would have them do unto you" sets a completely different tone for our day. Cutting folks slack when they express their stress undeservedly toward us is a gift to them and to us as well.

In the heat of any stressful moment, our minds speak out of the data available to them. Just as we don't expect polished English from those who can't read, so, too, Christlike responses do not come from those who seldom fill their mind with his teaching. "Junk in equals junk out" is a true adage.

If we read the teaching of Jesus and then meditate on it, the Holy Spirit has an opportunity to bring us understanding. This process is more than starting our day with a devotional reading. It is turning the words over and over as we go through our day. Then, at times least expected, the Spirit breaks through, helping us understand and apply what we have been reflecting upon. The goal is to know what Jesus said and make it a part of our lives. If we renew our minds with the words of Jesus, the things of God will come naturally. Thinking, loving, and living as Jesus requires input. It is more than data entry. It is absorbing and living out what he said. Stopping reflex reactions, which happen faster than we can think, involves a lot of new input as to how we think and what we believe.

Reaching for the Unreachable

Throughout the Sermon on the Mount, Jesus set the standard for how his followers should live. Phrases like love your enemies, turn the other cheek, go the second mile, and blessed are the persecuted set what appear to be unreachable goals. Christ in us is the means of living this way. While living among us, Jesus exemplified all of the standards he taught in how he lived. His strength to do so while in the flesh is available for us. The indwelling peace of God overcomes our selfish outcry of life not being fair. His assurance that the path we are on leads to something far better gives us the ability to walk as he walked, knowing that our present circumstance is not home.

The apostle Paul was in anguish about doing the very thing he did not want to do. In his struggle, he called out for deliverance. The answer came: "Thanks be to God through Jesus Christ our Lord!"

For God has done what the law, weakened by the flesh, could not do. By sending his own Son in the likeness of sinful flesh and for sin, he condemned sin in the flesh, in order that the righteous requirement of the law might be fulfilled in us, who walk not according to the flesh but according to the Spirit. . . . You, however, are not in the flesh but in the Spirit, if in fact the Spirit of God dwells in you. Anyone who does not have the Spirit of Christ does not belong to him. . . . For if you live according to the flesh you will die, but if by the Spirit you put to death the deeds of the body, you will live. (Rom. 8:3–4, 9, 13)

Placing our faith in Jesus and living by the Spirit is God's will for our lives. In Christ, we are transformed. We become new creations by spiritual rebirth. Through a maturing process, we listen to the Shepherd, stay attached to the vine, and are taught by the Spirit. Maturing in the Spirit happens only if we have a true heart's desire. Additionally, our desire must be matched with a willingness to train our faculties to be sensitive to the indwelling Spirit of God. Unless we develop the discipline of yielding to the Holy Spirit instead of our self-spirit, everything gets shut down.

Volumes can be written describing life in the Spirit. Many components work together for Spirit life to increase. Life in the Spirit is experience-based. Each incremental step of participating in the spiritual dimension of being in Christ brings the desired result closer to maturity.

A Word of Encouragement

Trying hard in our own power to be good is not how Spirit life works. Being empowered by the Spirit allows us to experience a supernatural way of life. This involves something happening to us, in us, and through us to the glory of God. It is how we respond to the One who said, "Come, follow me."

CHAPTER 10

APPROPRIATE LEVEL OF RESPONSE

Martyrs set the bar high for what it means to follow Jesus. Others seek the minimum response that they presume will still guarantee their place in the afterlife. Jesus set one standard for everyone: unless you deny yourself, take up your cross daily, and follow him, you can have no part in him.
—Ed Malone

WITHIN THE RANKS OF THOSE IDENTIFYING AS BEING Christian, the level of commitment to Jesus varies greatly. Many consider the call to follow Jesus as being more than is required. The mindset of many can be summed up with the following: "As for me, I believe in God and try to live a decent life. I am a law-abiding citizen, a good neighbor, and I work diligently to provide for my family. When it comes to Christianity and church, I am certainly not a fanatic. I take a more reasonable approach to all things in life."

The foregoing statement considers some response, but not an all-out commitment to Jesus, as being more than enough while guarding against excessive involvement. Granted, there are many things in life not deserving of over-the-top enthusiasm and devotion; however, there are things that merit an unlimited response. Is commitment to Jesus one of them? A good place to start in answering this question is with the New Testament writings.

Peter

After the ascension of Jesus, Peter's role in the church emerged quickly. It was at his suggestion that someone be chosen to replace

Judas. At the event of Pentecost (the outpouring of the Spirit), Peter addressed the crowd. Later, Peter's boldness to preach the resurrection of Jesus was accompanied by miracles. Peter was arrested, beaten, and, at times, experienced miraculous release from jail. When Philip took the gospel to the Samaritans, Peter went to check things out. Paul, in the letter to the church at Galatia, speaks of visiting Jerusalem early on in his ministry. He talks with Peter to be assured that he was not out of line with what Jesus taught. Peter's experience with Cornelius, a Gentile who received the Spirit just as the Jews did, was a major influence on the early church accepting Gentiles into Christianity.

Turning to Peter's writings, what does he emphasize as central to following Jesus? Did Peter's last thirty years cause him to water down or change what he heard Jesus teach? Following Jesus, even unto death, comes out as an undeniable message in 1 Peter. Throughout Christian history, many have used 1 Peter as a manual for how to live in the face of persecution. For Peter, how far one goes in commitment to Christ knows no boundaries.

> In this you rejoice, though now for a little while, if necessary, you have been grieved by various trials, so that the tested genuineness of your faith—more precious than gold that perishes though it is tested by fire—may be found to result in praise and glory and honor at the revelation of Jesus Christ. Though you have not seen him, you love him. Though you do not now see him, you believe in him and rejoice with joy that is inexpressible and filled with glory, obtaining the outcome of your faith, the salvation of your souls. (1 Pet. 1:6–9)

Peter accepts that trials, even unto death, may come. He assures his readers that their faith will be sufficient to stand the test. He commends his readers who, even though they have not seen Jesus, love him and rejoice with an inexpressible joy, being filled with God's glory. Loving Jesus and rejoicing with inexpressible joy is no casual response to our Lord.

In 1 Peter 2:20–21, Peter offers quite a challenge: "But if when you do good and suffer for it you endure, this is a gracious thing in the sight of God. For to this you have been called, because Christ also suffered for you, leaving you an example, so that you might follow in his steps." For Peter, it is a reasonable expectation that all believers follow in the steps of Jesus, whether the path is uphill or down, in sunshine or in rain. Doing good and suffering for it, as a gracious thing in God's sight, is a level of commitment hard for many to accept.

Peter writes, "His divine power has granted to us all things that pertain to life and godliness, through the knowledge of him who called us to his own glory and excellence, by which he has granted to us his precious and very great promises, so that through them you may become partakers of the divine nature, having escaped from the corruption that is in the world because of sinful desire" (2 Pet. 1:3–4).

Peter's assessment of what it meant to follow Jesus is quite challenging. First, it is by God's divine power that we have life and godliness. The goal is nothing less than God's glory in becoming partakers (sharers) of the divine nature. The intention is that all reach beyond the natural state of their existence by participation with God. Peter continues his thought with the challenge to make every effort in accomplishing this. Failure to do so is to be ineffective and unfruitful in the knowledge of our Lord Jesus Christ and to be blind to the fact that we were cleansed from our sins.

If you are looking for someone to agree with a laid-back, more reasonable approach to being a follower of Jesus, Peter is not your advocate. His response to such a proposal would be that you are blind to the glorious opportunity available in Christ. Some might label Peter a fanatic, while others see in him an appropriate level of commitment to the One he loves.

John

John lived until around AD 100. His ministry continued beyond Peter and Paul by more than thirty years. By the end of his life, he had had sixty years to process the meaning of what Jesus taught. As an interpreter of Christ, he set forth the level of commitment he felt was appropriate for all who seek to follow Jesus. As we look again at what John wrote, we can easily determine how he viewed commitment to Jesus:

> And by this we know that we have come to know him, if we keep his commandments. Whoever says 'I know him' but does not keep his commandments is a liar, and the truth is not in him, but whoever keeps his word, in him truly the love of God is perfected. By this we may know that we are in him: whoever says he abides in him ought to walk in the same way in which he walked. (1 John 2:3–6)

John's summation of what it means to follow Jesus presses us to examine whether we know Jesus and are in him or are just making the empty claim that we are. If we know him, we will keep his commandments, and doing so will not be a burden. However, we cannot follow his commands unless we know what he taught. Furthermore, we will not keep his teaching unless we pursue what he commands as the source of life.

John states that the certainty of whether we abide in Jesus is demonstrated by walking in the same way Jesus walked. The ability to do this is by the anointing of the Spirit, which enables what we cannot fulfill on our own. John overwhelmingly joins Peter in calling for a radical devotion to the One we love.

Paul

The apostle Paul was the most prolific writer of the New Testament. Many consider him the premier interpreter of Christ. Paul's conversion occurred after the death and resurrection of Jesus. He was taught by the Spirit. He stands as an example of what Jesus promised to be the role of the Spirit in the lives of all believers. Space does not permit highlighting all that is contained in the writings of Paul about commitment to Jesus. The following list highlights the major points he makes about following Jesus; it will be easy to discern what is expected, and in turn, we must ask ourselves if we meet the level of commitment he presents as the norm for all followers of Jesus.

1. Phil. 3:8, 10–11: "I count everything as loss because of the surpassing worth of knowing Christ Jesus my Lord. . . . that I may know him and the power of his resurrection, and may share his sufferings, becoming like him in his death, that by any means possible I may attain the resurrection from the dead."

   Is Paul being fanatical about following Jesus? Why would he be willing to commit to this level of pursuit of Christ Jesus? For Paul, Jesus, as Lord of his life, had delivered him from his ineffective ability to do what he should toward God while avoiding the things he hated. He had found a relationship with Jesus as the meaning of life, surpassing all that life had to offer. The call to suffer, and even to die, was not too much to ask in his quest for resurrection to the next life.

2. Col. 3:17, 23: "Whatever you do, in word or deed, do everything in the name of the Lord Jesus, giving thanks to God the Father through him. . . . Whatever you do, work heartily, as for the Lord and not for men."

   Is this even close to your way of life? I remember one Sunday, as we were leaving church, one of my parishioners asking, "Does Jesus have to be involved in every part of our lives?"

   My response was, "Why wouldn't you want him to be?"

   Some want Jesus as Lord to guarantee their place in heaven, but otherwise want the freedom to live the way they choose. To do so is to think that Jesus as my Lord will not lead me to life. It is saying that there is fullness of life outside of the bounds of what Jesus sets as appropriate for our lives.

3. Gal. 2:20: "I have been crucified with Christ. It is no longer I who live, but Christ who lives in me."

   In what way is the living Christ expressed through you? The miracle of Jesus flowing through us as branches attached to the vine is what Paul is referencing in this verse. It happens when we yield the right-of-way to the indwelling Spirit. The phrase "Jesus is not looking very good on you right now" is often what people see rather than the glory of Christ being properly expressed to our world.

4. Eph. 3:20–21: "Now to him who is able to do far more abundantly than all that we ask or think, according to the power at work within us, to him be glory in the church and in Christ Jesus."

   What lessons have you learned in utilizing the power of God at work within you? Where are you in the battle between your self-spirit's desire and the Holy Spirit's desire being expressed through you? Can you point to victories over the lies of the devil? Are your knee-jerk reactions being replaced with purposeful actions honorable unto your Lord? Has your sensitivity to the presence of God increased such that there is a new level of peace and control in your life? Is God glorified by how you live?

5. Rom. 12:2: "Do not be conformed to this world, but be transformed by the renewal of your mind, that by testing you may discern what is the will of God, what is good and acceptable and perfect."

   Do you blend in easily with the way of the world? What insights have you acquired as to discerning the will of God for your life? The renewal of your mind requires new input to overshadow old habits and dishonorable thoughts. Are you storing away movie lines or the Word of God in your heart? When situations press you, will your thoughts arise out of the storehouse of God's Word or out of the self-protecting mindset of our culture?

6. 1 Cor. 3:1–2: "But I, brothers, could not address you as spiritual people, but as people of the flesh, as infants in Christ. I fed you with milk, not solid food, for you were not ready for it."

What is your spiritual age? What is your spiritual diet? To say that you have been a Christian for twenty-five years is not an indication of your spiritual age. It is like doing carpentry for ten years. All many carpenters know is what they learned in the first year. For them, they have one year of experience ten times. What indicators are there in your life that demonstrate progress in your maturity to the fullness and stature of Christ? Does your regimen of spiritual training demand protein in your diet, or is milk more than enough fuel? As a growing Christian, do you crave to eat everything in sight?

7. 2 Cor. 5:17, 20; 6:1: "If anyone is in Christ, he is a new creation. . . . We are ambassadors for Christ, God making his appeal through us. . . . Working together with him, then, we appeal to you not to receive the grace of God in vain."

What, in your life, distinguishes you as a new creation? Some only want the grace of God as it touches upon going to heaven. God's desire to mature us into the image of his Son is not something they want. What God desires to give rather than what many want to receive stands miles apart.

The message of Peter, John, and Paul describing commitment to Jesus is ignored by many and rejected as being over the top by others. What we think, what we do, how we do it, and for whom we do it is wrapped up in what these followers of Jesus label as the only response fitting for the One who gave all that we might live. It is the response of love without boundaries.

Normal Christianity

Throughout the history of Christianity, individuals have come on the scene calling for renewal in the proper level of commitment to Jesus. Many folks, who claim to be God's people, fall in love with the world and are drawn after earthly pursuits. They find other things more important than the opportunity to have a relationship with God.

One of these voices calling for an appropriate level of commitment to Christ was an evangelist and writer in China during the 1930s. His name was Watchman Nee. *The Normal Christian Life* is a book that brings together the messages he wrote in tracts and magazine articles for twenty years. The book opens with this statement: "What is the normal Christian life? We do well at the outset to ponder this question. The object of these studies is to show that it is something very different from the life of the average Christian."

Watchman Nee maintains that when the apostle Paul defines what it means to be a Christian, he is not stating something special or peculiar like a higher level of Christianity, but he is presenting God's normal for all Christians.

Learning to participate with Jesus as our Shepherd, experiencing the flow of the Spirit, being taught by the Spirit, and maturing in the fullness of the in-Christ relationship is not just for the elite. It is normal Christianity. It is what prepares us to hit the ground running in the next life.

Only through the fullness of Spirit life and the devotion of love without boundaries will the true meaning and purpose of life be accomplished. This level of all-out, first-above-all-else response to God is normal Christianity. Jesus taught that once you see God's kingdom, you will give everything to have it. When you do, life moves to a new level.

Considering the magnitude of God's desire for a relationship with us and for us to be spiritually prepared for eternity, how is it not worthy of our total commitment? Jesus taught in Matthew 6:24, "No one can serve two masters, for either he will hate the one and love the other, or he will be devoted to the one and despise the other." A priority choice and commitment are required for Jesus to be our master. We often speak of something being the opportunity of a lifetime. The expectation is that we should not let the moment pass. By all means, we should do whatever it takes to seize the opportunity. What Jesus offered stands light-years above anything one might pursue in this life—it is the opportunity of eternity!

Mature in Christ

One final emphasis for this chapter is a Scripture passage we have already touched upon, found in Colossians 1:27–29: "To them God chose to make known how great among the Gentiles are the riches of the glory of this mystery, which is Christ in you, the hope of glory. Him we proclaim, warning everyone and teaching everyone with all wisdom, that we may present everyone mature in Christ. For this I toil, struggling with all his energy that he powerfully works within me."

Paul's consuming passion, to which he applies all the empowerment God gives him, is to present everyone mature in Christ. It is unthinkable that many who claim a place in Christianity are not aware of or even care about whether they are mature in Christ. The spiritual dimension of life is dismissed. Paul's passion was fueled by what he understood to be the meaning of life. If we are shortsighted in our view of life, earthly pursuits will be what we reach for.

The scope of what Jesus offers is the opportunity of eternity. If the opportunity of a lifetime demands no price too high to pay, what should the opportunity of eternity command?

A Word of Encouragement

Both the Old and New Testaments call for loving God with all of our heart, soul, mind, and strength. Is to do so an over-the-top response, or is it the level of commitment deserving of our Lord and Savior?

CHAPTER 11

If I Had Known

Jesus said, "Come, follow me." The extent to which one follows has been an age-old question. Failure to meet the standard he expects has eternal consequences.
—Ed Malone

FINDING YOURSELF IN A PLACE, NOT KNOWING HOW YOU got there or what is going on, is quite disturbing. The room I was in was crowded with people waiting for their turn to speak with an individual seated at a table up front. Frantically, I looked around, searching for something to help me figure out the nature of my situation. How did I get here? What is going on?

After a few moments, I caught the attention of the one seated next to me. Trying not to let my anxiety show, I made a joke about my dilemma. "I must have taken a wrong turn because I have no idea of what's going on. What is all of this about?"

When he turned to respond to me, I could see a look of panic on his face, and he was constantly shifting his feet back and forth. "Don't know," he replied. "But for sure, all of this makes me feel uneasy."

Out of the corner of my eye, I noticed a lady seated a couple of rows over to my left. She was hard to ignore because of her radiating smile and what seemed like a glow about her. Getting her attention was not going to happen since she was completely enraptured in the moment. She was not the least bit bothered, and in fact, she looked as if she could hardly wait for her turn up front.

There had been a steady flow of people to the front of the room. Each one seemed to know, in some strange way, when it was their turn. My anxiety was building. Nothing within range of me was giving any indication of the nature of my circumstance.

Life's Interviewer

As time progressed, I found myself closer to the front, without knowing how I got there. This new position allowed me to hear bits and pieces of the conversation at the front table. The interviewer had a file folder for each person, which he consulted from time to time.

The noise in the room lessened, enabling me to listen to pieces of the conversation at the table. I heard the interviewer say, "I need to figure out how to fit you into what we have going on." He picked up the file folder and started to look inside, but then laid it down and said, "Rather than read the report, just tell me what strengths and abilities you have to make available to us."

The guy at the table had an athletic physique and a definite air of confidence about him. I strained to hear as he made his response. "Obviously, you are not aware of who I am. Folks say I was the best to ever throw a football."

The interviewer interrupted him, saying, "Throwing footballs doesn't fit into what we do here. Don't you have something else worthwhile to offer?"

The guy at the table almost came out of his chair. "Something more worthwhile to offer! I want you to know that I was paid millions of dollars to do what I do." The noise level of the room heightened, blocking out the rest of their conversation.

Before I realized it, a new person was at the table. What caught my attention was that the file folder for this gentleman was very thin. The countenance of the interviewer was quite subdued as he opened the file. With only one piece of paper to review, the interviewer said, as if speaking to himself, "There are still some openings in the nursery."

The fellow at the table was not overpowering at all, and in fact was the kind of guy who could blend into a room without being noticed.

However, at this point, he spoke up: "Did I hear you correctly? Did you say something about the nursery? You need to know, I'm not very good with children."

Without even raising his head, the interviewer responded, "That is because you are one."

At this point, I realized that the file folder was a record of how each person had lived. It functioned as a type of résumé, helping the interviewer find the appropriate placement for each person for what lay beyond the room. It was not about what they had accomplished, but rather who they had become. How much money they had made, what kind of house they had lived in, or the prestigious positions they had held were not in the record. The focus was on the person's values and the driving ambition of their life. It was a picture of the person's heart as demonstrated by how they had lived.

The next interview was over quickly. The interviewer showed the individual that in his file was a blank sheet of paper without even his name on it. The interviewer explained, "This means that no one here knows you. You don't show up on any of our records." The one being interviewed raised his voice and shook his fist in anger, but was quickly removed from the room.

The lady with the radiating smile was next to approach the table. Her file folder, packed as full as possible, was handed to the interviewer. Quickly, he set the folder aside and came forward, meeting the lady as she approached. They hugged and smiled and greeted one another as best friends. Others came out to meet her. All I could hear amid the excitement was, "Well done, well done!" as they escorted her out of the room.

Things settled down, and a new person was at the table. The interviewer was first to speak. "As I look through the file, there is not a lot in here to work with, but we do have a training program to help you get up to speed."

The one at the table was quite exasperated. "There has to be some kind of mistake. Are you sure that you have the right file? I am abundantly qualified and can fit into anything you might have going on."

The interviewer answered, "We get a lot of folks like you who are what we call professional spectators. They love to watch, but don't often participate. They enjoy hearing about what we do, but they seldom get involved. With at least an appreciation for our mission, you are trainable, but it will take time."

My turn was quickly approaching. Will my file be thick or thin or even just contain a blank sheet of paper? It was becoming hard for me to concentrate. I could sense my pulse rate and blood pressure rising as I waited for my turn at the table. Before I realized it, I was sitting on the front row. I could hear clearly what was going on at the table. The one being interviewed said, "If I had known this is how things were going to work, I would have lived differently. I would have made it my priority to be ready for what you have going on. I would have concentrated on being a better person rather than just striving for stuff."

The interviewer started to consult the file, and as he reached for it, he said, "Perhaps you are one of those who lived where no instruction manuals were readily available. Some have a very limited exposure to what they should be about in their daily living to prepare them for this day."

The one being interviewed said, "No, sir, I had a copy of the manual. In fact, I had several. However, I did not read them. I am ashamed to say that I did not take seriously the true meaning of life. My cues for how to live and what to pursue came as a result of blending into the way of life around me." Expressing genuine shame and sorrow, he continued. "If I had only known that this day was coming, if I had taken the time to read the book, if I had responded to the inner pull I felt instead of allowing the drumbeat of my world to overshadow it, I would be seated here today prepared. I am truly sorry."

Before the interviewer responded, I awoke from sleep. I was wet with sweat, my heart was pounding, and my mind was racing; it took a moment to collect my thoughts. Was it only a bizarre dream or was it a warning graciously extended to me by my Father?

At various times, Jesus spoke about the next life with his disciples. He assured them that he would return to take them to the place being prepared for them. In the interim, he expected them to be about the work of the kingdom. Being faithful over what he left us to do gives the opportunity for service ahead. On the other hand, failure to live responsibly bears eternal consequences.

Rich Man

In Matthew 19:16–22, Jesus was approached by a young rich man. He asked what he needed to do to inherit eternal life. Jesus told him to keep the commandments. The rich man asked, "Which ones?" Jesus listed several for him, and the young man assured Jesus that he was spot on in following them. However, sensing that there was more to it, he asked, "What do I still lack?" Jesus told him, "If you would be perfect, go, sell what you possess and give to the poor, and you will have treasure in heaven; and come, follow me" (vv. 20–21).

What the man possessed actually possessed him; it was his god. To be perfect means that the young man had not completed the process of allowing God to be his Lord. When Jesus told the rich man to keep the commandments, his response of "Which ones?" reveals that he felt some commands were optional. The instruction of Jesus to keep the commandments was not an invitation to pick and choose, but to follow all that was given.

The encounter with the rich man prompted Peter to say, "See, we have left everything and followed you. What then will we have?" (Matt. 19:27). Jesus told the disciples that they will sit on thrones in the new world, not as a privilege, but rather for usefulness in continuing to serve the One they love. The response of Jesus to Peter pictures the next life as being a place of service. The ability to serve the One we love is contingent upon preparation and participation in the things of God. The treasure in heaven Jesus promised the disciples will not be things to consume upon themselves, but will be the pleasure of being equipped to serve their Savior, Creator, and Lord.

Laborers in the Vineyard

As an extension of this conversation, Jesus gave the parable of hiring laborers to work in the vineyard, which is recorded in Matthew

20:1–16. The first group was hired at the beginning of the workday with an agreed payment of a denarius. Others were enlisted to work, starting at different times throughout the day. They were promised to be paid whatever was right. At the end of the day, all received a day's wage. The first group hired felt cheated.

All the workers had been in the marketplace seeking the opportunity to put bread on the table for their family. Those hired later in the day expected to receive less than what they needed. In the end, they were given grace. The first group hired, instead of being happy for those who were going home with enough to feed their families, complained. For them, the opportunity to work had begrudgingly turned into bearing the heat of the day. Jesus told them that many who are first will be last, and the last first.

Consider what it would be like to stand in the marketplace each day waiting for the chance to work. Think of what it would be like to make the trip home empty-handed. Even after several hours pass, there is still the faint hope of being hired; at least there would be something rather than nothing for your family. With three hours left in the workday, though, all hope is gone. Frantically, you begin searching for a way to deal with your situation. If you were hired unexpectedly, how would you feel? How hard would you work without complaining? Surely, with joy and appreciation, you would give your very best.

One of the main points of this parable centers on the grace of God. Like the opportunity to work, God gives us the opportunity of life. He was under no requirement to create life. He certainly was not obligated to give the level of freedom we enjoy. The freedom to be truly alive and self-determining creates circumstances that God must endure as a result of our choices. It was his plan that we would give our freedom back to him as our Lord.

God not only gives life, but he gives the means to eternal life as well. His grace is beyond compare. Serving the One who blesses us so richly should not be a chore. It should be our heart's desire. Being thankful for what God has given will show in how we live.

Selfishly, we can possess life as if it belongs to us. We can pursue fun and pleasure and complain when there is not an opportunity for more. Like our children, we can live expecting the good life without appreciating or even noticing the sacrifices made to provide it.

The second focus of this parable involves the response of the first group hired. Having experienced days when they were not hired or were only given a few hours to work, they should have rejoiced with those receiving the grace of a day's wage that enabled them to feed their families. However, they were focused on themselves and how they should receive more than what they agreed to work for. As a result, they felt as if they had been wronged. Their blessed opportunity to work negatively morphed into their inability to rejoice with those blessed. All of this revealed a lack of thankfulness for the opportunity given to them.

If I were a day laborer blessed with work, no task would be too hard or beneath me. The joy of being able to feed my family would supersede any difficulty or discomfort. I would do all in my power to be a blessing to the one who blessed me.

The laborers hired first were not thankful. They did not rejoice with the blessing the others received. Instead of being thankful, they felt that they deserved more. We must be certain that we rise above the mindset of these laborers; otherwise, it will be hard to fit us into what is going on in the next life.

Ten Maidens

Jesus gave additional teaching in Matthew chapter 25, strengthening the concept of being properly prepared for what lies ahead. In the parable of the ten maidens, Jesus pictured a group of maidens preparing to attend a wedding.

The custom of the day was for the groom to finish the living arrangements for his bride and then go to get her. Five maidens prepared as they should have by bringing oil—not to be left in the dark if the groom delayed his coming. The other five were not as diligent in their preparation; therefore, when the groom was later than expected, they could not go out into the dark to meet him. During the time it took for them to purchase oil and arrive at the wedding venue, the door was shut, and they were not allowed in. It is alarming to consider that they wanted to go to the wedding, but inadequate preparation shut them out. Wanting to go to heaven, like wanting to go to the wedding, demands more than a casual desire. The five who brought oil just in case it might be needed were seriously intent on not being left out of the celebration, no matter what happened.

This same level of commitment about being sure one is part of the kingdom of God is demonstrated when Jesus answered the question of only a few being saved: "Strive to enter through the narrow door. For many, I tell you, will seek to enter and will not be able" (Luke 13:24). The Greek word translated as "strive" is *agonia*. Going from Greek to English, we get *agonize*. If one agonizes to enter the kingdom, it is certainly not a casual desire, but an all-out effort to reach one's goal.

Sheep and Goats

Jesus pictures the end of life as also being like a shepherd separating sheep from the goats. Two groups are formed. Placed in one group were those who helped the hungry, thirsty, naked, strangers, sick, and those in prison. The other group consisted of those who ignored these needs in others. The first group was gathered into eternal life, and the second group into eternal punishment.

This parable of separating the sheep from the goats is a clear statement that responses of the heart to the needs of others matter. It is the kind of person who fits into the next life. God's plan to give us a new heart and a new spirit evidenced by loving others is required for those living in his kingdom.

Talents

The parable of the talents, also in Matthew 25, strongly presses that how we live in this life determines our usefulness in the next. Jesus tells the story of a man who went on a journey. He called his servants and entrusted them with his money. Each was given a portion according to their ability. His money was divided into five talents, two talents, and one talent. A talent in today's market would be in the range of a million dollars.

After a long time, the master returned and asked for an account of their stewardship. The first two had doubled their portion. To each the master said, "Well done, good and faithful servant. You have been faithful over a little; I will set you over much. Enter into the joy of your master" (Matt. 25:21, 23). By proving to be a faithful servant while the master was gone, they would be entrusted with greater responsibilities in the future.

We have been given life, abilities, and opportunities, which the Father entrusts to us. Jesus said in Luke 12:48, "To whom much was given, of him much will be required." For many, each day is consumed with just being able to put food on the table. Those living in abundance have a greater responsibility to meet the needs of others. We can consume all life has to offer upon ourselves, or we can give our lives back to God to accomplish his purpose through us.

The servant who had one talent was unfaithful. He hid the talent in the ground, bringing back only what he had been given. This servant was declared to be a worthless servant and was cast into outer darkness.

We have been entrusted with the gift of life. In the end, will we stand before our master with only what we were given? Symbolically, like the worthless servant who buried the master's money, have we hidden the gift of our life in the things of the world? God is trusting us to invest our lives in things heavenly, not earthly. His intention is for us to multiply what we were given. If we prove faithful over little by losing our lives for the sake of the kingdom, he can trust us to be faithful over much in the life to come.

There are many ways to multiply the effect of our lives for the sake of the kingdom. Being a servant to others belongs at the top of the list. The ability to walk in unconditional love is how we serve. Those with a servant's heart and a servant's lifestyle are the kind of people the Father desires to be with him. If we mature as a conduit of the Spirit to others, being able to be taught by the Spirit, then knowing and following the Shepherd's voice prepares us for endless opportunities ahead. If we can be trusted to put God first and demonstrate the willingness to follow his commands, our usefulness to the Father is wide open. If we demonstrate that we have been conformed to the image of his Son, then God's investment in our lives has accomplished the goal he intended.

God's gift to us of life was costly. He has endured the result of our freedom being used wrongly. His investment to redeem us from our wrong choices and the opportunity to extend to us eternal life was costly. Yet the goal he has for us out of his great love is worth the cost.

It is sad when you trust someone, only to have them prove unfaithful. Your expectation and desire for them painfully crash around you. It breaks your heart. On the other hand, when those entrusted prove faithful, it is one of the greatest pleasures of life. It is no small thing for the Master to say to the faithful servants, "Enter into the joy of your master" (Matt. 25:21).

With joy, God wants to say to everyone, "Well done, good and faithful servant. You have proven trustworthy with the life I gave you by investing yourself in that which is heavenly. Even without eyes to see what lies ahead, you have yielded to my pull on your life and to the things that have shaped you. Your response to my desire for you brings me joy! Come, follow me! We have an endless future of things yet to be done as we continue to walk together."

Your Turn at the Table

Returning to the allegory at the beginning of this chapter, we are faced with some important questions. If you were at the interviewer's table, what would your file folder look like? What would the record of your life demonstrate? Are you ready to hit the ground running in the next life? Have you become who you need to be?

Some might respond to all of this by saying that as far as my file folder goes, it will simply have a big stamp on the outside saying, "A sinner saved by grace." Certainly we are all sinners saved by grace. The point being discussed is not the basis of salvation, but rather our response to it. The file folder is not about earning points with God. Apart from the vine, we can do nothing. The file folder is a record of our thank-you notes to the Father for the grace he bestows on us in life and salvation. Every point of denying ourselves, taking up our cross, and following Jesus is how we say thank you. It is giving back what has been so freely given to us that God's desire might be fulfilled through us. By committing ourselves to Spirit life, we express the desire to interact with and be a channel of the Father's love in our world.

When our file folder reaches the interviewer's table, it will be clear whether our thank-you is just words. A life lived to the glory of God demonstrates being truly thankful. Those with thankful hearts are God's kind of people. They will have no problem finding a place in the next life.

Priceless Pearl

The determining factor in all of this is the value we place on the kingdom of God. Jesus said in Matthew 13:45–46, "Again, the kingdom of heaven is like a merchant in search of fine pearls, who, on finding one pearl of great value, went and sold all that he had and bought it."

Like all of us, the merchant had been going about his daily activities trying to figure out how life works and his place in it. Possibly he had worked several different jobs. For him, making a decent living and securing his financial future were daily concerns. Eventually, he settled into buying and selling pearls. With a keen eye for a good deal and knowledge of how to market pearls, he established a way to make his living.

One day he found a special pearl. It was not an ordinary pearl, but one such as he had never seen before. Its value was priceless. Without question, it was the most valuable thing he had ever seen. He could only buy it if he sold all he had. The choice for him was clear.

Jesus would have commended the merchant's ability to recognize the pearl's value and his willingness to sell all to have it. However, Jesus would have said to him, "For what does it profit a man if he gains the whole world and loses or forfeits himself?" (Luke 9:25). There is more to life than a secure financial future. Unless steps are taken to provide for our souls, then all is lost. The Kingdom of God is priceless. He who has eyes to see will sell all to participate in it. The kingdom is for those who recognize that to live under the rule of God surpasses all life has to offer. It is the meaning and purpose of life.

The question is, what will the record show describing who you have become? Living a God-empowered life yielded to Jesus as our Shepherd is the proper response to his gift of grace. Doing so should not be hard unless there are things in life that we deem more desirable. Even now, learning to listen to his voice and being taught by the Spirit allows the Father to plug us into what he is doing in our world.

Denying your selfish spirit and walking in the ways of God is a thank-you card the Father enjoys reading. Make it your aim to drop God a note of thanksgiving each day.

The transition to the next life should be something we think about often. In some fashion, there will be a process assessing if, how, or where we will fit into what is going on there. Through spiritual maturity and loving unconditionally, we are available for a wider scope of responsibility. Many people just want to get to heaven, even if it is just by the skin of their teeth. For them, availability and response to God now or in the future do not matter. God's intention for creating our world being realized through them is not important—just wanting to go to heaven may prove to be not enough. In the parable of the ten maidens, all of the maidens wanted to go to the wedding. However, for five of them, wanting to go was not enough. Failure to heed the warning Jesus gave with this parable can be a huge mistake with eternal consequences.

A Word of Encouragement

"Come, follow me" is an invitation to an out-of-this-world opportunity that fulfills the meaning and purpose of life. It is required that you go through a narrow gate and along a path pursuing what only a few find worthy of their life.

CHAPTER 12

TAKE US HOME

Followers of Jesus, through a supernatural relationship with him, experience a foretaste of their true homeland. Jesus leads, and we follow, to an otherwise unattainable goal of finding our way home.
—Ed Malone

ON ONE OCCASION WHILE SERVING IN THE MILITARY, I volunteered for a flight over North Vietnam. I was not the pilot, but was the one responsible for identifying the target and coordinating artillery firepower. Our aircraft was a fixed-wing, single-engine Cessna with front and back seats and dual controls.

After some time in the air getting a feel for the lay of the land and flight maneuvers, the pilot said, "I've been shot; the plane is yours." He wasn't shot, but was placing me in a situation that could realistically happen. In fact, on the day before, we had lost a plane and its crew.

Quickly, I keyed my mike: "This is my first mission. I know nothing about keeping this plane in the air."

As the plane began to fall, the pilot said, "Grab the wheel and push and pull on things until you get a response. Do something, do anything, before we kiss the ground!" His final instruction was, "Take us home!" As a military officer, being pitched into deep water with the expectation to swim was not unusual. This time it was different. Although I was in an unexpected training session, the seriousness of the moment pressed upon me. I realized that my mock situation could quickly become a reality.

My pilot left me to myself. He made no response to anything I said. My plea for additional help yielded no response. The silence was deafening. It was clear that I needed to slow my brain down and take a deep breath. We were still two thousand feet in the air, giving me room to figure something out.

As you might imagine, I was all over the place. The instrumentation needed to reveal whether the plane was rising or falling was up front, visible by looking over the pilot's shoulder. It didn't take long to realize that my movements needed to be slow and cautious. I needed to feel what the plane was doing in response to my actions. Above all, I needed to stay high in the sky, allowing room for recovery from any panic reactions in moving the controls. As long as I didn't let the nose of the plane drop and maintained sufficient engine speed, I was not going to plunge out of the sky unless we ran out of fuel. A quick look at the fuel gauge revealed a full tank. Once I could maintain the plane in a stable pattern, I began focusing on finding my way back to our base camp. I knew that traveling north or west would put us in harm's way; therefore, pointing the aircraft in a southeasterly direction, I kept my eyes fixed on the landscape looking for Dong Ha. Once I caught a glimpse of the Ben Hai River, separating North and South Vietnam, I knew that my combat base was only seven miles away. When the airstrip came into view, I lined up on the runway. At this point, the pilot took control of the plane and we headed back to our original mission to the north.

With the airstrip behind us, the pilot keyed his mike all excited and said, "See, you did it! Even when you thought you couldn't, you brought us home."

To which I responded, "All I did was enable us to die at home instead of some remote piece of dirt in North Vietnam. I would have killed us both trying to land."

"Oh no," he responded, "the guy in the control tower would have brought you in."

I did not share my pilot's confidence that the one in the tower could have gotten me home safely. That's a lot to believe about someone you've never met and know nothing about. Trusting someone to help me do something that places my life on the line is not an easy sell. To this day, I remember looking at the runway, adjusting my grip on the wheel, and wondering what my next step should be. When the pilot took control of the plane, it was a much-welcomed relief. My alarming experience in the plane that day has always been an analogy of life for me.

More to Life

At the point we realize that there is more to life than what we see, and when we sense the greatness of the created order, we are forever changed. Although life offers moments of fun and excitement, nothing compares to the wonder behind our world that beckons to us. For some, understanding and getting in touch with this pull becomes a larger-than-life priority. They see it as the purpose and meaning of life. In turn, it makes life here seem less like home. Folks with this perspective about life begin looking at the horizon, hoping to get a glimpse of what lies beyond. There is a longing within them that nothing in life satisfies.

Thinking in these dimensions provides the setting for Jesus to meet us on the path we are traveling with an invitation: "Come, follow me; I can take you home. You will learn how to follow as we travel. Our journey leads through a war zone. The path is narrow and requires effort to stay on course. At times, your inward insecurity will rebel against following someone you can't see to a place you have never been. Spending time together on this journey will lead to experiences that surpass all life has to offer. Our destination is more than you could ever imagine. You have sensed its pull on you, but you have no idea of what lies ahead. Life there will be different. Throughout our journey, you will be changed. The world you are presently living in is specifically designed to shape you for the life you are longing for."

It is alarming to me that professing Christians face the transition to the next life with fear rather than with desire and anticipation. Some long for home, while others hold on to this life with every ounce of energy they have.

Landing Safely

Returning to the illustration of my flight experience in Vietnam, Jesus functions as the one in the control tower ready to bring us home safely. For an untrained individual to land a plane, several things need to happen. First, fear and uncertainty must be pushed back to allow concentration. The decision to completely trust the guy in the control tower is mandatory. Listening to each instruction and responding immediately is critical. At no point can the untrained pilot do his own thinking. If the plane is yielded totally to him, the one in the tower will land the plane. Yielding my life to Jesus in this way is what assures a safe arrival home. Jesus will do it through me. He does what I cannot do myself. When I am yielded to him, he will take me home.

To you, my reader, I am like the pilot who had complete confidence that the guy in the control tower would be able to bring me on in. My pilot knew the guy in the tower. They lived together at the airstrip. They had many flight experiences together. The confidence my pilot had rested on personal, real-life experiences with him. I can assure you, based on my personal experience with Jesus, he is more than capable and can be trusted completely to take you home. Indeed, he is the only way to make it home.

Where Is Home?

The question is, where is home? The writer of Hebrews speaks of those who feel like strangers here and, therefore, are seeking a homeland. They desire a better country. After being on a trip and heading home, sights, sounds, and smells begin to fill our minds. Thoughts of the hugs, smiles, and warmth of meaningful conversation begin to fill us with excitement. Home is a special place. It is the place where you belong and feel loved. It is a treasured place.

Once our sense of home lies beyond this world, who will you trust to show you the way? How will you make a safe landing in the place where your heart longs to dwell?

While in Vietnam, I shared living quarters with six helicopter pilots. When in the air, I was often given control of the chopper.

Maneuvering a fixed-wing or rotary aircraft after takeoff is not that difficult. Autopilot is a feature on many planes that does the flying for you. However, when it is time to land, everyone wants the aircraft in the hands of an experienced pilot.

When I think of life analogous to flying, the landing part is when life here ends. Having never passed through the event that leads to the next life, we are faced with a task beyond our capability. Trusting, yielding to, and welcoming the hands of the Master at the wheel of our aircraft is what will enable a safe landing.

Putting Your Weight Down

The story is told of the farmer who was invited by his grandson to take a plane ride. Upon returning from the flight, grandpa was asked what he thought about the experience. He responded, "I never put my weight down." On the farm, when attempting to cross a mud hole, success is achieved when you don't put your weight down all on one foot. Grandpa's commitment to the flight was less than total commitment. If we make it home, we must put our weight down. We must be totally committed and fully surrendered to Jesus, allowing him to take us home.

It has been fifty years since my flight experience in Vietnam. The impact of that event has stayed with me strongly. I remember vividly looking at the runway and wondering how I would survive if this was real. Among trained pilots, 50 percent of fatalities occur during takeoff and landing. The chance of survival in my situation would have been extremely low.

In parallel with Spirit life, the gate is narrow, the way is hard, and few find the life offered by Jesus. Some never put their weight down in full commitment. Others are unwilling to surrender control of their life to anyone.

Living through You

The analogy of the guy in the control tower landing the plane through me is an excellent picture of life in the Spirit. The way life in the Spirit works is by Jesus doing things through us. When I suited up for the plane ride, I was given a helmet that allowed for communication with the tower, my command center, and the pilot. Spiritually, the communication process is accomplished without a special helmet. The emphasis spiritually is on feeling rather than hearing.

When God visits us at the level of conscience, we feel his press upon us. Without words, there is the certainty of his authority beckoning us to reevaluate our actions and attitudes. When we focus on his presence, there is a level of peace and comfort that fills our soul. As we learn to be taught by the Spirit, we stay constantly sensitive to his input that comes as a by-product of thinking about the things of God. The response of the Spirit comes at times and in ways not expected. By not filling our minds with the junk of this world, there is an opportunity to be taught. By the discipline of pulling away from the stress and noise of life, we can center our thinking on the things above.

Feeling the press of his authority, the peace of his presence, and thoughts inspired by the Spirit establishes pathways for communication. When something is said that we feel is unfair, our default mechanism is to defend and counterpunch. If we work in the realm of the Spirit, much is available to guide us to a different outcome than our knee-jerk reactions of self-defense. When faced with an obstacle in our flight pattern, Jesus stands ready to take over the controls. However, if our response is made quickly, our self-spirit grabs the controls and fires away with an aggressive reaction. Our rockets are deployed, and every piece of available firepower is engaged. Once the smoke clears, death and destruction line the battlefield. As a result of our actions, we are left to rebuild the relationships that we have destroyed.

The outcome can be different if we let Jesus fly through us. At the first hint of anger, God presses his authority upon our conscience. If we are accustomed to sensing God's authority and the peace of his presence upon our actions and reactions, an early warning system will be engaged before things go too far. Once we feel the coldness of losing God's favor, our soul cries out to change course. Saying and doing nothing is usually the best course of action. Waiting for how to respond in the Spirit assures us of not having to walk amid destruction later. Listening rather than responding produces an entirely different perspective. When this is going on, Jesus flies the plane of our life, giving us time to slow our minds down and breathe.

The flight described from my time in Vietnam was not a mission where a target was already identified. Our mission was to be available to the ground troops in the area who might need additional firepower when under attack. Our job was to come to their aid.

Spiritually, we are in a flight pattern of being available to God for support and assistance to those in need. Clear communication is essential in order to respond when called upon. A constant input of music, talk radio, movies, and earthly endeavors can easily drown out transmissions from the command center.

I have found that one of the great benefits of writing is that I am constantly, day and night, spinning thoughts around in my head of how to best shape the flow of my thoughts. I am not worried about the election, my investments, or whether my favorite sports team will achieve victory. Instead, my thoughts are absorbed in expressing the message of the kingdom. As a result, my Spirit life is heightened greatly. As I seek inspiration and critique for what I am writing, I am carried into the presence of God. Working with the Spirit as I write is a wonderful experience. At times when I read to edit my efforts, it feels as if I am reading something that someone else has written.

Some might consider my comments, at this point, to be weird and even bridging upon some type of psychological disorder. However, for those who follow Jesus, it is how we fly with someone else at the controls.

Take Us Home

When my pilot called for me to take us home, I was more than willing to go. Flying over hostile territory is not like taking a ride in the country and enjoying the scenery. If God were to tell us beforehand that it was our time to go home, what would our response be? Facing the prospect of his life ending, Paul said, "For me to live is Christ, and to die is gain. If I am to live in the flesh, that means fruitful labor for me. Yet which I shall choose I cannot tell. I am hard pressed between the two. My desire is to depart and be with Christ, for that is far better" (Phil. 1:21–23). For many people, it seems as if they have more holding them here than they have drawing them to the next life.

Paul told Timothy that the time of his departure had come. The word he used means to cut a ship loose from the dock. Ships were built to be set free to sail the sea. For Paul, his life was a ship built by God that was now ready to be cut free from the dock to make the trip home. He could speak of death with excitement, anticipating life in the next world that would not be lived in a combat zone. He was ready to continue serving his Lord in this new dimension of life.

His longing for home is expressed clearly in his letter to the church at Corinth: "We know that while we are at home in the body we are away from the Lord, for we walk by faith, not by sight. Yes, we are of good courage, and we would rather be away from the body and at home with the Lord. So whether we are at home or away, we make it our aim to please him" (2 Cor. 5:6–9).

Paul's goal for living would be the same whether he was here or in the life to come. He aimed to please the Lord. A change in where he lived would not mean a change in the passion of his life. As a recipient of the grace of God, he had a heart of thanksgiving expressed by his desire to please the Lord.

The desire of Paul's heart was to please the Lord. Do you know the Father well enough to be certain of what pleases him? Is your life one big shooting-from-the-hip, or do you take careful, purposeful aim at pleasing the Lord?

The elder John wrote to the church, "I have no greater joy than to hear that my children are walking in the truth" (3 John 4). I'm sure that the same would be true for God about his children.

Eager Anticipation

There are not many things in life that I enjoy more than strapping on my tool belt and joining a crew on a building project. I find great pleasure in being able to contribute to the completion of a project.

In the same vein, I look forward with great anticipation to the time when I arrive in the next life ready to join the project God has going on. I want to do more than carry lumber or hand tools to the one doing the work. If I have allowed God to train me and I know how he does things by having worked projects with him, I'll be ready to join the team with the Master Carpenter in the lead; it is the aim of my life, whether in the body or present with the Lord.

Lesson in Spirit Life

My flight experience in Vietnam demonstrates the many ways in which the Spirit can teach us. In Scripture, we find numerous occasions of God using ordinary events to teach spiritual truth. God told Jeremiah to go to the potter's house for the message he wanted to give him. Jeremiah had seen clay being thrown all of his life, but now this common event would be his teacher. In like fashion, Jesus used the everyday occurrences of a man sowing seed, a pearl merchant searching for pearls, and the Spirit being like the wind to reveal spiritual principles. There are times when God can use most any event in our lives as our teacher. Our natural existence and the spiritual realm have much in common as they share the same Creator. By only living on the surface of life, we often pass by moments that can be the vehicle of truth. Our world is uniquely designed to achieve God's purposes. As we live, we can simply focus on consuming the creation or being consumed by the Creator. The choice is ours.

A Word of Encouragement

The fullness of life is a continuing journey—not a destination. I pray that enough has been given to guide your willingness to follow Jesus. Be certain that God's people are stationed throughout the world. Surround yourself with true followers who will help, inspire, and learn with you in the fullness of following Jesus home.

CHAPTER 13

TEST TIME

Examine yourselves, to see whether you are in the faith. Test yourselves.
Or do you not realize this about yourselves, that Jesus Christ is in
you?—unless indeed you fail to meet the test! (2 Cor. 13:5)

What Will You Do with What You Have Read?

We are all familiar with test time. Having completed training and academic requirements, individuals from various professions sit for qualifying exams. Simply being exposed to the training is not sufficient for being awarded a license. Engineers, doctors, nurses, pilots, and a host of others are tested to give assurance of their competence. Whether it is the ACT, a driver's test, final exams, or a professional license, anxiety builds considering the future possibilities that passing the test allows.

Whether we are in the faith by Jesus being in us is the most important question of life. Since Jesus said, "Not everyone who says to me, 'Lord, Lord,' will enter the kingdom of heaven" (Matt. 7:21), we know that more than a lip-service commitment is required. Paul's challenge is quite unexpected when he tells the church at Corinth, "Examine yourselves, to see whether you are in the faith. Test yourselves" (2 Cor. 13:5). How is self-examination a fair evaluation? Why would Paul suggest such a strange concept?

The test of being in the faith centers on matters of the heart. Those around us cannot know with certainty what is in our hearts because it is beyond their reach. Without the ability to know us at our inner being, they can only take us at our word. When it comes to faith, many are actors playing a role proclaiming something that is not true. Jesus said to the scribes and Pharisees, "So you also outwardly appear righteous to others, but within you are full of hypocrisy and lawlessness" (Matt. 23:28). With certainty, God knows the genuineness of your professed commitment to him.

The need for testing rests on the fact that many believe they are part of God's people when they are not. Those calling for the crucifixion of Jesus were part of a strong religious tradition. Before his conversion, the apostle Paul and others with him pressed for the death of Christians, believing it was a mission given to them by God. There seems to be no limit to the level of misunderstanding surrounding matters of faith.

The Required Standard

Micah called for doing justice, loving kindness, and walking humbly with God (Mic. 6:8). Jesus said, "If anyone would come after me, let him deny himself and take up his cross daily and follow me" (Luke 9:23). Personal evaluation of whether these statements capture how you live and who you are is not outside your ability to know.

Making the choice to follow Jesus is a journey, a relationship, and the fullness of life. Fishermen left their boats, sacrificing everything. Martyrs have followed Jesus even unto death, and yet some who claim to be Christians know nothing of his teachings or how he lived and have no desire to live in a relationship with him. Their focus is only on what will happen after they die. A wide gap separates the level of commitment many believe is sufficient in responding to Jesus.

Scripture declares it a lie to say you know Jesus and abide in him when you do not follow his commands and live as he lived. The difference in knowing Jesus and knowing about him bears eternal consequences.

To walk as he walked is a tall order. Followers of Jesus know that even with his indwelling power, their lives pale in comparison to his. Striving to live as he lived remains the goal. He joins us in our quest, carrying us to heights unattainable on our own. The question of whether we endeavor to live as he lived must not be ignored.

New Way of Life

Jesus presented a new way of life for those seeking to live as he lived. Jesus spoke of being born again, of sheep hearing the voice of the shepherd, of a branch abiding in the vine, and of the Holy Spirit as teacher and guide. In this new way of living, sensing and feeling take precedence over hearing and seeing as the followers of Jesus learn to feel his guidance as it comes wrapped in his presence. Life in Christ involves something happening to us, in us, and through us to the glory of God. Whether or not you are experiencing the power of the Spirit being expressed through you is not beyond your ability to know.

Paul speaks of the Spirit bearing witness with our spirit that we are children of God, enabling us to call out to God as our Father. This is one test of the faith that all must pass. Calling God "Father" is different from having him as *your* Father by honoring him with your life. Paul assures his readers that no one belongs to Christ unless they have the Spirit of Christ dwelling in them, confirming God as their Father.

Test Questions

John, in his first epistle, emphasizes repeatedly the importance of knowing if you abide in Christ and he in you. John is not alone in his concern. As stated above, the total witness of Scripture reveals that many are self-deceived about matters of the faith. We have addressed these Scriptures already, but repeat them here as they are extremely important in addressing if Christ is in us:

> And by this we know that we have come to know him, if we keep his commandments. Whoever says "I know him" but does not keep his commandment is a liar, and the truth is not in him, but whoever keeps his word, in him truly the love of God is perfected. By this we may know that we are in him: whoever says he abides in him ought to walk in the same way in which he walked. (1 John 2:3–6)

No one born of God makes a practice of sinning, for God's seed abides in him; and he cannot keep on sinning, because he has been born of God. By this it is evident who are the children of God, and who are the children of the devil: whoever does not practice righteousness is not of God, nor is the one who does not love his brother. (1 John 3:9–10)

Whoever keeps his commandments abides in God, and God in him. And by this we know that he abides in us, by the Spirit whom he has given us. (1 John 3:24)

It is obvious that many of John's readers believed and proclaimed that they were in God when their lives failed to substantiate their claim. This is an important warning to all who profess Christianity. John's statements are abundantly clear, needing no additional commentary. It is critical that each of us examine ourselves in light of the truth he gave.

Awake from Sleep

All around the world, many are presently reliving the days of the book of Acts by embracing the good news of Jesus in the face of intense opposition. The report from the persecuted church is humbling. Christianity is establishing a strong footing in many places throughout Asia at the cost of many lives. Even with the oppressive power that China holds over its people, God has birthed a movement there despite attempts to extinguish it. In many places in Africa as well, there are expressions of Christianity that will not be denied, even amid persecution.

All of this is happening among those of faith who are willing to die rather than renounce their commitment to follow Jesus. On the other hand, Christianity in America is falling asleep. Entertainment, hype, lights, and crowds, accompanied by the shallowness of the preached word, assures that our expression of Christianity will soon be void of its power to change people's lives.

I fear that the American expression of Christianity has evolved into an empty religion of benefits to receive without the call to deny ourselves, take up our cross, and follow Jesus. Short of a spiritual awakening, American Christianity cannot be guaranteed protection from what many in the church have endured since the first century. If America were faced with the ultimate test of our faith, do we have warriors prepared to take their stand in the battle, or are we producing spectators not willing or prepared to fight the good fight of the faith?

Three Simple Words

These words spoken by Jesus, "Come, follow me," have changed the lives and revolutionized the world of countless people. It involves more than embracing his body of teaching as being true. It is to make his words our way of life. We are not left to struggle on our own trying to understand and implement abstract concepts. We follow a person who comes alongside us in our journey. He is the example, the helping hand, and the encouragement needed to walk in this new way.

Because of Jesus, we see our world in a brand-new light. It is the opportunity to join hands with our Creator, Savior, and Lord, walking out his cosmic purpose. Our world is a classroom for the angels and principalities to observe the manifold wisdom of God. It is a workshop that molds and shapes us for an eternal purpose. It is the place where we embrace the need by faith to give up our personal freedom in exchange for living under God's rule. It is a call to rise above the surface level of living.

The magnitude of what we are offered in Jesus supersedes anything else life has to offer. Martyrs are proof of that being true. What about you? Has following Jesus changed your life and revolutionized your world as you seek to live as he lived, fulfilling the Father's will?

The essence of testing yourself to see if you are in the faith centers on the question of whether you have a heart-centered commitment to God expressed in how you live. It is to acknowledge that we are living in a temporary world leading to an eternal future. We are called to a present change in who we are and how we live so that one day we can arrive at home mature in Christ.

Full Circle

In bringing things to a close, it is important to return to where we began. In the opening pages of this book, a critical question was posed: Has the modern expression of Christianity evolved into yet another man-made, lip-service expression of religion?

The question raised was based upon the history of the Judeo-Christian journey that reveals a constant departure from God's intention for his people. The call of the prophets to realign to God's will, the ministry of Jesus setting the correct standard for what God desires, and the Protestant Reformation string together the ongoing issue of man-made religion replacing a heart-centered and life-yielding connection with God. In recent years, significant shifts have occurred in defining our faith and calling as the people of God. Are we on course? Are we achieving the goals Jesus set for us?

The level of commitment Jesus called for was nothing short of radical. He pointed those around him to a priority love for the Father that knows no boundaries and has no rivals. When called upon to give, family relationships and life itself are not too much to give when living in God's kingdom. Unapologetically, Jesus called for his followers to pursue God's kingdom above all things in life. His invitation to deny ourselves, take up our cross, and follow him daily looms over those seeking only the minimum level of response that assures them a place in the next life. Believing something about Jesus and attending a church meeting is a far cry from living with him in a present spiritual relationship by yielding to his lordship over our lives. Whether each of us is genuinely participating in what Jesus called us to is the question that merits our complete and undivided commitment. The content of this book stands as a means for you to know personally the standard Jesus set that will give us abundant life into an endless future.

A Word of Encouragement

"Come, follow me" is an invitation to an out-of-this-world experience that fulfills the meaning and purpose of life. It is my prayer that you will go through this narrow gate pursuing what only a few take seriously and find worthy of their life.

ORDER INFORMATION

REDEMPTION PRESS

To order additional copies of this book, please visit
www.redemption-press.com.
Also available on Amazon.com and BarnesandNoble.com
Or by calling toll-free 1-844-2REDEEM.

CPSIA information can be obtained
at www.ICGtesting.com
Printed in the USA
BVHW041809150322
631532BV00011BA/785